KV-611-331

"*Iraq Through a Bullet Hole* is a book long overdue, primarily because the media has provided us with insufficient coverage of the Iraqis' viewpoint regarding the overthrow of Saddam Hussein and the American occupation of their country. Issam Jameel has come forward to reveal his experiences in his native Iraq, a country he left many years ago, but returned to in 2005 to mourn his nephew's accidental killing by an American soldier. Jameel does not express his opinions on the war, but reports impartially on events and conversations he witnessed and partook in regarding the crisis within his homeland. The strength of Jameel's story lies in his ability to remove himself from the situation while his background provides him with a more knowledgeable understanding than the Western media, not ingrained in Iraqi culture, can achieve."

—Tyler R. Tichelaar, PhD

"In *Iraq Through a Bullet Hole*, Jameel shows in a brutally honest fashion the deconstruction of the infrastructure in Baghdad since the fall of Saddam, as well as the splintering of once peaceful communities into hostile religious factions. He also gives a personal, eyewitness picture of the effect the new environment had on his kinfolk, especially how his nominally religious family had turned toward radical and strident forms of Islam as a way of giving meaning to their daily struggles. The anger and hurt that many of his relatives had comes through clearly. Disappointments, loss of security, fear, worry and empty future fill almost every page of Jameel's hard-hitting story."

—Michael Philliber, PhD for *Reader Views*

3033622

UNIVERSITIES AT MEDWAY LIBRARY

Iraq
Through
A Bullet Hole

A Civilian Wikileaks

Issam
Jameel

Book #5 in the Reflections of History Series

Iraq Through A Bullet Hole: A Civilian Wikileaks
Book #5 in the Reflections of History Series
Copyright © 2011 Issam Jameel. All Rights Reserved.

No part of this publication may be reproduced, transmitted in any form or by any means, electronic, mechanical, photocopying, recording, or otherwise, or stored in a retrieval system, without the prior written consent of the publisher.

Library of Congress Cataloging-in-Publication Data

Jameel, Issam, 1954-
    Iraq through a bullet hole: a civilian wikileaks / Issam Jameel.
        p. cm. -- (Reflections of history series; bk. 5)
    ISBN-13: 978-1-61599-090-0 (trade paper: alk. paper)
    ISBN-10: 1-61599-090-9 (trade paper: alk. paper)
    ISBN-13: 978-1-61599-091-7 (hardcover: alk. paper)
    ISBN-10: 1-61599-091-7 (hardcover: alk. paper)
    1. Jameel, Issam, 1954- 2. Iraqis--United States--Biography.
3. Jameel, Issam, 1954---Travel--Iraq--Baghdad. 4. Jameel, Issam, 1954---Travel--Iraq--Mosul. 5. Iraq--History--2003- I. Title.
    DS79.66.J36 A3 2008
    956.7044'3092--dc22
    [B]
                                                    2010031094

Published by:
Modern History Press, an imprint of
Loving Healing Press
5145 Pontiac Trail
Ann Arbor, MI 48105
USA

http://www.ModernHistoryPress.com or
info@ModernHistoryPress.com
Fax +1 734 663 6861
Phone 888-761-6268

Modern   History   Press

The Reflections of History Series

My Tour in Hell: A Marine's Battle with Combat Trauma by David W. Powell

Made in America, Sold in the 'Nam: A Continuing Legacy of Pain (2nd Ed.), by Rick Ritter and Paul Richards

More Than A Memory: Reflections of Viet Nam, Ed. By Victor R. Volkman

F.N.G., Revised Ed. by Donald Bodey

Iraq Through a Bullet Hole: A Civilian Wikileaks by Issam Jameel

From Modern History Press

"Those who cannot remember the past are condemned to repeat it."

—George Santayana, *Life of Reason* (1905)

Table of Contents

Photographs

The photo shown on the book cover was taken in December 2004. The view is Al-Rasheed Street, one of the main streets in Baghdad. Photo taken by Ghassan (an Iraqi photographer). Used with permission.

Additional photographs were supplied by Bill Evans, a civilian telecommunications contractor in Iraq during 2004.

Introduction

I never even thought of writing a diary during my last visit to my motherland, Iraq, after having been away from it for twelve years. I found myself in such a dangerous situation that I suffered a state of shock that rendered me unable to write, or even to note down any remarks, because I was overwhelmed by the thought I might never leave Iraq alive. But after I arrived home safely in Australia, I realized how important it was to record what I had seen. I have endeavored to record my experience without judging people. I tried to stay as a witness for the events I had seen, the people I had met, and the dangerous times I had passed through, observing and feeling the pulse of life in Iraq. This book is a way to understand some of the important issues in Iraq, which are not easy to grasp by people elsewhere who can only follow media reports.

When I started to write in English, I was not sure whether I would be able to complete this work, but day by day, I have seen myself approaching closer and closer to my goal. Writing this book has been a wonderful experience for me, not only because of the opportunity to record a critical time in my life, but because it is the first book I have written in English.

However, I must acknowledge people who helped me to finish this book, especially Ms. H. Salmon, who expended a great amount of effort for this book. Ms. Salmon was with me from the early drafts, revising and teaching, and I am greatly indebted to her. I also owe a great deal to her family who welcomed me into their home with true Christian hospitality.

Also, I express my gratitude to Mrs. Babbage, who helped me in revising some chapters.

Finally, I have to state that the some of the names of

the people mentioned in this book have been changed in order to protect their privacy and ensure their safety.

—Issam Jameel
November 2010

| **1** | **Arrival** | |

Iraq-Jordan border: June 26th, 2005

It was 1:30 a.m. when our four-wheel drive finally drew close to the border Jordan shares with western Iraq. For someone flying from Sydney, Australia, to visit his mother country after having been away from it for twelve years, there was a sense of both gravity and adventure. The car had three rows of seats. I shared the rearmost one with a young Jordanian man, while in the middle seats were an Iraqi boy of about twenty in front of me, a tall Iraqi young man, and a bald Iraqi man on the left side. The front seats were occupied by a Christian Iraqi lady in her fifties along with the stumpy young Iraqi driver.

During the travel from the Jordanian capital, Amman, I attempted to avoid any dialogue with my fellow passengers, who were seizing on any chance to talk. Normally, I like to talk to people, but this time, I thought it might lead me to disclose my nationality. I had been warned by my wife and so many friends, not to reveal my Australian nationality to strange people. Many stories had been spreading in the Iraqi community—stories about people of Iraqi background with foreign passports being kidnapped during their visits home. For this reason, I held an Iraqi passport in addition to my Australian one, which I'd placed in my pocket. I had planned to use the Iraqi passport to gain entry into Iraqi territory, due to the dangers threatening foreigners, especially Australians, since Australia was, and still is, one of the countries in the military coalition with the United States of America.

The serious part of the trip hadn't begun yet; we had to drive about seven hundred kilometers before reaching Baghdad. Indeed, this road is the most dangerous part of this trip, for many military incidents occurred on it. As a result, the traffic had been stopped many times during the year before my visit. Many horrible stories concerning this road came to my mind. They were not fictitious stories, but real ones transmitted by many TV channels, or by various persons, telling how many people had been attacked and killed on this road. Also, many foreigners were kidnapped and had disappeared. The passengers who accompanied me didn't show much concern for the coming danger, but I was able to read the inescapable destiny imprinted on their features, in spite of all their attempts to hide it.

* * *

The car slowed to a stop, for we were at the Jordanian border office. I'd had to pass through this isolated place twelve years ago, when I had left Iraq. I never conceived that one day I would have to come this way again, and I never imagined that Saddam Hussein's regime could be changed, or that I would be able to return to Iraq. But here I was again, standing in an office where they stamp the passports. It was in a one-room timber portable building.

The other passengers finished all the procedures and left the office, while I stood at the counter, waiting to solve my problem. The Jordanian officer told me that I should pay a fine of about three hundred American dollars because I didn't have a residency stamp in my Iraqi passport. That was when I realized that I'd made the mistake of not transferring the residency stamp from the Australian passport onto the Iraqi one.

"You can use your Australian passport without paying any fine," he said. Because I wasn't able to afford that amount of money, I had to go through the immigration procedures as an Australian. I held out my passport and gave it to the officer, who stamped it with the departure date. I looked over my Australian passport, thinking that all my attempts to hide my nationality were now gone with the wind.

Iraq: June 26th, 2005

We left the Jordanian border behind and pressed forward into Iraqi territory. While we passed under the big archway where the cars can go through to the Iraqi border, I noted the absence of the huge picture of Saddam Hussein that used to be in front of that arch.

It must have been destroyed or damaged after the collapse of Saddam's regime, I thought.

As our car edged cautiously along the narrow, twisted track, we could see some American soldiers at the other end, at the checkpoint. Some passengers asked the driver to reduce his speed, even though he was driving very slowly. The woman in the front seat looked at him and cautioned: "If you move too fast, they might shoot at the car."

These few words were enough to put fear into my bones, but there was no way to retreat; I had to go forward.

When the car stopped at the checkpoint, I was able to see the features of the American soldiers suspiciously watching the passengers. It was the first time I had ever seen real American soldiers, not just in the movies.

After they checked our passports, one of the soldiers tried to be friendly, when he observed that the woman in the front seat was wearing a cross around her neck. "Are you Baptist?" he asked, but she was silent, for she couldn't understand English.

I was looking through the right hand window at a soldier. *It's going to be really hard work when the soldiers ask us to take our heavy luggage out to be checked*, I thought to myself. But the soldiers gave the order to the driver to move toward the office, where the passports were stamped. I was taken aback, wondering why they

didn't ask us if we had something to declare in our luggage.

A gas station and restaurant waited on the left side of
the main road, about five hundred meters beyond the
checkpoint. The car drove off the main road to queue with
the many other cars that were already waiting to fill up
with gas.

As soon as the car pulled up, the driver told us to stay
inside for safety. A few minutes later, I realized he was
right, when a quarrel broke out nearby. A thin man with
dark brown skin was trying to get somebody out of the
back seat of a car next to us. Some people gathered
round to have a look, while the person inside the car
struggled to stay there. When the thin man couldn't haul
him out, he began to boot him savagely, while some other
men tried to drag him from the other side of the car. I was
looking at the weary, unconcerned faces of the people all
around, who were watching it as a familiar scene. Eventually, the man in the car gave in, so they were able to get
him out and took him away, forcing him to go with
punches and slaps. This was the first sinister sign, and I
could have predicted what would be in the wind.

It was now 2:00 a.m., but the place was crowded with
people from everywhere. There were drivers, passengers,
and some people called *Bahaara* (Arabic for marine). I
found out later that this is what Iraqi people call those
who smuggle and sell gas illegally; they were buying gas
from remote gas stations to sell in the large cities at high
prices, or to smuggle it to Jordan. I wondered why they
were called *Bahaara*, since they were very far from the
sea. *Maybe they got this name as most oil smuggling is being done via the sea at Al-Basra port, in the south of Iraq*, I
thought.

Sitting in the car all this time was enough to make me
bored, so that when some of the passengers got out, I did
too. I was watching the slow movement of the long line of
cars at the gas station, thinking of the beaten man. *He*

might have been one of the terrorists, I thought, when the thin man again emerged from the restaurant. He walked very proudly, explaining what had happened regarding the beaten man, though nobody asked him: "He thought that there was no law, forgetting he is now in an Islamic country," he said. "He was trying to buy a beer in the restaurant!" He began to proclaim the new system in Iraq, which was now based on Islamic law (*Shariat*).

He kept talking about the new rules in Iraq while I was able to look at his dirty, creased clothes as he came closer.

What a poor beaten man, I said to myself, thinking that if the beaten man had been punched and slapped just for asking to buy a beer, what would have happened if he had drunk it?

Meditating on the now unknown destiny awaiting me depressed me deeply in my soul, so that I needed to be alone. I moved to the side, thinking of the thin man: *Who is he? Is he an agent working for Iraqi intelligence working in the border office?* Over the past twelve years, I'd kept on dreaming about the day of liberation, and finally liberty had come. But what had been the outcome? The intelligence agents in Saddam's time had secretly arrested and persecuted many people, but now people were persecuted in public, and just for thinking of a can of beer!

* * *

The time passed by as lazily as the forward movement of the cars in the gas queue. I looked toward the restaurant and thought it would be good to have a cup of tea, but a mysterious foreboding obsessed me and made me reluctant to move far from our car. But the desire to break free from a fear-bound state simultaneously propelled me toward the restaurant.

Once I reached the restaurant entrance, I realized that it would have been good to follow this sense. It was as if something from the depths of my soul had tried to warn me.

A crowd of people rushed toward the restaurant from many directions, looking for a place to hide. Meanwhile, the shouts of American soldiers were heard behind. All this mixed eerily with the sounds and the red glow of bombs lighting up the sky. In a few seconds, everything became chaos and people were rushing everywhere. I found myself running with the others, looking for a safe place to hide, with no time to think or ask what was happening. Some of the crowd dashed into a dirty bathroom that was adjacent to the restaurant. I followed them, but the stinking smell pushed me out. Then I turned around the corner of the restaurant, following some other people who had entered into the kitchen, using the rear door. About eight people went in there, and I was one of them.

We stood still in the kitchen, waiting for the situation to calm down and watching what was happening outside through a window in the wall, normally used to deliver food to the restaurant dining hall. A few seconds later, a short American soldier rushed into the restaurant hall by the main entrance. "Get out! Get out!" he shouted angrily, pointing with his machine gun. All who were in the kitchen understood that we should use this window to get out. Meanwhile, nobody had the courage to retreat, or to use the rear door of the kitchen. One by one, we climbed through the open space into the restaurant hall. The soldier was watching every move, with fear and nervousness engraved on his face. He pointed with his gun, indicating that we had to leave the restaurant. Thus, we passed among the restaurant tables very cautiously, while I observed the soldier's features as closely as I could. He was a short man, with blue eyes in an oversized head.

Outside the restaurant, a huge crowd of people were besieged by several soldiers aiming their guns toward us. The short soldier with the big head gave orders to get us to line up. I tried to be as slow as I could, dragging my feet so as to remain at the back.

About sixty men were queued up in three lines. I was

at the edge of the third line. I also kept myself near the restaurant entrance so that, in case the soldiers started to shoot, I would be able to take cover in there. Indeed, it was a very dangerous situation, because the soldiers were ready to shoot any time, and any wrong movement would have been a stimulus strong enough to kill us all. I looked at the people who were lining up with me, seeking to share my emotion with them in those horrible moments, but I was surprised when I saw indifference on their faces.

What kind of people are these? I thought and I sensed that I did not belong with them, even if they were Iraqi.

The American soldiers began to check every person's face against the photo on their identification document. I guessed that they might have been looking for a particular one, or making sure that none of those people had crossed the border illegally.

One of the soldiers spent a long time questioning a young villager without papers. "Show me your ID... your ID!" the soldier repeated many times, but the villager was unable to understand English. I spoke up, explaining the meaning of "ID" to the villager, so the soldier invited me to interpret. I left the line to approach the villager and began to interpret. I could observe the young villager accurately while he was talking. He was a rather lanky man, wearing a long and dirty traditional shirt. I perceived from his accent that he hailed from the western part of Iraq, a fact confirmed by his story.

He said that he had lost his identity document two weeks ago and he was trying to get another one but the procedures were very complicated. When the soldier asked him what was he doing here, the villager replied that he was selling gas and that was his job. The soldier didn't seem to believe the villager's story, so he took him apart from the other people, while another soldier came to photograph him with a digital camera.

I turned back to my line, thinking about the villager's

story. Actually I didn't believe what he said either.

How could anybody roam in this dangerous area without identity papers? I thought, remembering that most of the people in the western part of Iraq had been involved in fighting the American army, and that the Americans were still suffering in this rebellious part of Iraq.

Acting as an interpreter gave me such a feeling of relief that some comfort began to creep into me. I realized that as an interpreter, I was privileged above the others, and that meant I might get preferential treatment. This proved correct when the time came to show my passport to the soldier.

"Are you Australian?" asked the soldier, checking my passport. Then he began to inquire about how long it took to fly from Sydney to Jordan, what was the reason to visit Iraq, and so on.

I also realized that I got an additional advantage from my nationality, and this made the conversation even friendlier, especially when the soldier began to inquire about Sydney's beaches and the beautiful girls. I was able to watch his eyes starting to glow when the conversation turned to the subject of women.

What made this soldier abandon the beautiful beaches of America to get in this remote desert? I wondered. Really, I felt sorry for him. He was a very handsome, tall young man, and he could get a beautiful American woman and share a peaceful, quiet life with her, instead of fighting in a strange, remote land.

Attracted by the friendly conversation, some other soldiers gathered, while the gaze of the surrounding people was beginning to penetrate and terrify me. I felt as if the people were staring at my passport. In a moment, all the scenes of kidnapping foreigners, which had been broadcast by countless TV channels, flashed through my mind, and suddenly, the feeling of relief disappeared, and I was struck by a terrible sense of fear.

Most of this rabble are terrorists, I thought, and then I

remembered that I must spend most of the night with these people, before the driver could start travelling again, because nobody dared to drive on that road at night.

"Would you please do me a favor," I said to the soldier, taking advantage of the friendly atmosphere. "I want to return to Jordan."

"Did we terrify you?" responded the soldier proudly, but I was too embarrassed to say yes.

"No, it's not about you, I just feel that I am in danger, I can't spend the night with these people," I said in a tremulous voice coming from my dry throat, thinking that I must leave this place by whatever means possible, and I was aware that I made a big mistake in coming back to my mother country in such dangerous times.

In any case, I didn't expect that the soldier would care for my request, but I quickly found that I was wrong. The soldiers showed alacrity in assisting me. Two soldiers accompanied me to our car, where my luggage lay in the back seat. They carried my heavy luggage around, looking for a car to drive me back to Jordan, while the eyes of the people followed us, filled with questions.

The soldier with the oversized head came along the main road. His head was turning in all directions, searching the area, and as soon as he noticed the soldiers carrying my luggage, he headed toward them. But before he could ask a question, the soldiers explained to him what was going on. It wasn't hard for him to comprehend my problem, and he showed great interest. He took charge of my situation himself and moved hastily forward, waving with his hand for me to follow him. I did so, wondering what he was going to do, when he stopped near a small Iraqi taxi parked near the restaurant.

"Get out," the soldier ordered the driver. So he got out of the car in terror. He couldn't understand the soldier's English ordering him to drive me to Jordan. In fact, I didn't want to find a car this way, so I interpreted the soldier's order as polite in manner. But the driver apologized. He said that he had come from Jordan and he couldn't turn back again.

Once the short soldier understood what the driver had said, he burst out angrily, demanding the driver obey the order. The driver looked at me and tried to apologize in a soft voice, so I turned to the big-headed soldier and asked him to find another driver.

"He will do it because of this," the soldier said and rapped on his gun.

"I don't want to force him. I want him to be happy to drive me," I replied quietly.

The soldier nodded his head approvingly and patted me on the shoulder.

"Good man," said the soldier, turning back to the main road.

I looked around for another car, but after a while, I decided that turning back to Jordan at this time was impossible. I remembered that all the cars travelling to Jordan had to leave Baghdad in the early morning to reach the border by evening.

I have to wait until tomorrow evening if I want to go back, I thought, realizing that I was stuck inside Iraq and must go on and finish this journey. I blamed myself for the hasty decision I had made to return to Jordan, so I retraced my steps to pick up my heavy luggage, when the tall handsome soldier approached again.

"Are you still willing to go back to Jordan?" he asked.

"No, I've changed my mind. It's too difficult to find a car to Jordan at this time," I said, trying to apologize to the soldier for the trouble I had caused him, but he was so kind and generous that he insisted on carrying my luggage back to the car.

When I returned, the queue had moved ahead and the car was close to the fuel pump. Most of the passengers were outside, except for the woman in the front seat. The passengers were talking about the driver, saying that he

UNIVERSITIES AT MEDWAY LIBRARY

wanted to leave the place and to park at Point Sixty, which meant sixty kilometers (38 miles) away from the border. I already knew that there was a restaurant there, where the drivers used to spend the night, when no car could drive beyond this stop at night.

In any case, I wanted to leave this place too because I wanted to get away from the rabble that had discovered my nationality.

But then, I wondered about the passengers who were to travel with me.

The young villager came in sight again, and some inquisitive people gathered to listen to his story.

"The Americans set me free," he said and turned to me. "Without your help I might have been in detention," he added, showing his gratitude to me for interpreting his pleas to the American soldier.

I tried to show him that I was pleased to hear this good news, but deep inside myself, I was surprised, thinking that the soldiers were very tolerant with this suspicious-looking person. The car was getting closer to the fuel pump, so the passengers got in and took their seats, while the Christian woman tried to calm me down, saying that what happened was just an accident.

"These things don't happen every day," she said.

The young boy in front of me seized the opportunity to reply to her with a joke. "Don't worry about him; he is working with the Americans as an interpreter." He laughed.

"You must be worth about twenty thousand dollars!" he said, turning his face to me.

I was very upset by this joke. It meant a lot of things to me because all the interpreters who worked with the American army were being treated as traitors by the radical Muslims. It was a common and lucrative practice in Iraq to kidnap interpreters for sale to radical groups. For this reason I realized that this joke could be blackmail in disguise, and that I should be more cautious.

Eventually, having refueled, our car moved toward the main road. We left the American soldiers behind, and our car passed through the darkness of the desert onward to an unknown destiny.

The driver went so fast across the dark wilderness that it didn't take long to reach the sixty Km mark. When the car arrived at its destination, there were a lot of trucks parked in the wide, open courtyard of a restaurant. It was a remote place located in the middle of the desert, where no city or even a village could be seen nearby.

The driver moved slowly and parked between the trucks; then he switched off the engine and rested his head back on the seat. "We'll stay here until dawn," he said, and with that, closed his eyes.

I wanted to get out of the car to sniff some air. Once I did so, a cool wind began to stroke my face, so I buttoned up my jacket. It was cool despite it being the end of June, when the temperature in Iraq usually becomes unbearably hot. But we were in the desert, where the temperature rapidly falls at night. Outside the car, there were so many small pebbles spread on the ground that I couldn't walk easily, but the white neon lights of the restaurant, which were filtering through the spaces between the trucks, helped me to find my way. In spite of all the fatigue I felt, I wasn't able to sleep. It was about 3:30 am, and there were still three hours to dawn. The Jordanian, with whom I was sharing the backseat, got out of the car too and came close to me. I was thinking of spending some time in the restaurant, but the fear of what was hiding behind the corner kept me dithering. At any rate, the Jordanian interrupted my hesitation when he invited me to join him for a cup of tea, and I felt safe enough to go with him.

Outside the restaurant, there was a wide concrete sidewalk where a crowd of people were lying on the ground, using dirty blankets underneath their bodies.

They might be drivers, I thought. The Jordanian led me to a small teashop beside the restaurant where a few people occupied some plastic chairs. We chose to sit down at a round table, while a young boy brought two small glasses of tea. I didn't worry about the people who were there because I was sure that nobody could recognize my nationality as my Australian passport was tucked away snugly in my jacket pocket.

The Jordanian tried to show his kindness and generosity by paying for both glasses of tea. During the entire trip, he was careful to show himself this way to the other passengers. I recalled what had happened as soon as we arrived at the Iraqi border, when the driver asked us to collect Iraqi currency to give a tip to the Iraqi guards before reaching the American checkpoint. The Jordanian had paid on our behalf two times and he refused to let us repay him. I interpreted this behavior as a reaction to the fear in his innermost self, and I perceived this fear even when we were on Jordanian soil, as he tried to show his loyalty to the Iraqi people in many ways. One of these was by declaring to the passengers that he was married to an Iraqi woman.

In fact, if truth be told, it might be difficult to explain his behavior without knowing the political circumstances in those times; that three months before my trip, a suicidal Jordanian man belonging to one of the radical Islamic groups exploded himself among a crowd of Iraqi people at Al Hillah city, eighty kilometers south of Baghdad. The majority of this town were Shia Muslims, which Sunni Muslims accuse of departing from the traditional Islamic faith. Thus, some radical Sunni groups believe that killing Shia Muslims is a sort of religious duty. 125 people were killed as a result of the Jordanian bomber's suicidal attack[1]. This event affected the diplomatic relations between Iraq and Jordan, when the media exposed the nationality of the suicide bomber, as well as broadcasting images of angry Iraqi people rushing into the

---

[1] "Iraq suicide bomb kills at least 125." *CNN World.* Posted 02/28/2005.

Jordanian embassy in Baghdad, destroying the furniture and tearing up the Jordanian flag. The reason for their anger was that the Jordanian bomber's family had proudly celebrated the death of their son in Jordan, declaring him to be a martyr.

Knowing all these details was very important to understand the fear of that Jordanian.

We were still making the usual talk about the hardship of this long trip and how many kilometers remained while the time passed slowly. In spite of all my exhaustion, I would have liked to stay at the teashop, spending the night under the white fluorescent lights, but the conversation began to make me weary and could only be continued at the cost of an increasing amount of effort, which made waiting very tedious. So I suggested spending the rest of the night inside the car.

When we got back there, the time was just a quarter past four. My eyes were blinking, unwilling to surrender to the exhausted lids. I didn't know what might happen if I went to sleep, so I kept awake, while everybody else slept.

It was still night when the driver woke up. He adjusted his position and scratched his eyes, before he turned on the car. It was half past five when the car began to move again, and this woke up all the sleepy-eyed passengers. I wondered why the driver had left the rest place early, when the darkness was still covering everything. Anyway, he seemed in a hurry. This stout fortyish driver was always in a hurry. The first time I met him, in Amman, the capital of Jordan, he had hastened to fill the vacant seats in his car, and sped to leave Amman in the early evening.

"If you had left Amman later that would have been better; we'd have arrived here in the morning," I said wearily. Some of the passengers assented, while the driver remained silent.

Most of the drivers start their trip from Amman to Baghdad at night, and they usually spend the night driving the five hundred kilometers between Amman and the Iraqi border. Thus, they arrive in Iraq in the morning to resume their journey to Baghdad in daylight.

It's my fault for choosing this car to travel in, I thought, while trying to suppress my frustration. Those moments took my mind back to the last week before my trip had begun.

I had procrastinated many times before making the decision to start the trip to Iraq. I used to pass by the travel agencies every day asking them how safe the road to Baghdad was, but the unpleasant stories that I heard always discouraged me.

In fact, there were many reasons that pushed me to brave the dangers. One was the bad news I had received regarding a nephew, my brother's son. He was killed by American soldiers by mistake. That was what I had heard when I called my sister from Jordan. I thought that my duty to console my brother for losing his elder son was more important than any risks.

However, with all the precautions that I had made to have a safe trip, I chose badly with this driver. I was looking out into the wilderness, wishing to meet a military unit or anything to indicate the existence of some government authority; but there was nothing, except the darkness of the horizon.

| **2** | **Traveling a Treacherous Road** | |

Western Iraq: June 26th, 2005

The features of the desert gradually appeared with dawn. The driver was rubbing his eyes repeatedly to banish the sleepiness from them. We were still crossing the long desolate desert, where no civilian life could be found.

This part of the road was the most dangerous because it was out of reach of any authority. For this reason, this remote place became the best location for smuggling and plunder, and to ambush passengers. I was looking to the wild flat land, thinking that no amount of troops or military detachments would be able to dominate this wilderness.

The boy in front of my seat got some medicines out of a plastic bag, while he began to talk about his illness. He said he was getting treatment with the assistance of a Christian charitable organization. Indeed, most of the passengers who accompanied me had been in Jordan for medical treatment. Because of the decrease in healthcare standards in Iraq, some voluntary organizations working in Jordan are now providing free medical care to Iraqi people[2].

The bald man in the left middle seat began to talk about his sickness too. He was complaining about the neglect in Iraqi hospitals, with poor treatment and corruption found everywhere. In a few moments, the conversation turned to the large numbers of casualties that

---

[2] Caritas Jordan provides medical aid to more than 300,000 Iraqi refugees living in that country.

hospitals are usually obliged to accept, because of the frequent suicide bombings occurring every day.

"All of them become martyrs. If anyone is killed by these bombers, he'll be a martyr," said the boy in front of me.

"Who said this!? This is nonsense," the lady objected. Of course, she was talking from a Christian point of view, which contradicts the Islamic belief. I expected a very heated argument there, but the passengers preferred to remain silent.

The car descended from the road to park at a rest stop with a restaurant, about 160 Km from the border (see p. 186, note #4). It was early morning, and the air was rich with humidity. The passengers got out of the car to have breakfast at the restaurant, while I preferred to have a cup of tea at a kiosk outside.

When I turned back to the car, the woman was still in it. As we were alone, the woman took the opportunity to talk with me freely.

"Foolish people; they are consoling themselves by believing foolish ideas about martyrs," she said irritably, and looked at me, waiting for my reply. In fact, her opinions about martyrdom accorded with my own belief, so I nodded. This encouraged her to go on.

"Are you from Baghdad?" she asked me.

"I was born there."

Having found somebody to listen to her, she vented her anger, as if she was against all that had happened. "You'll find a lot of foolish people when you arrive in Baghdad. It is not the same Baghdad you dream about, everything has changed," she said in (insert 'a') frustrated voice. "The Shia religious parties have dominated Baghdad, as well as the other cities," she whispered. I thought she might guess from my Iraqi accent that I wasn't from the Shia Muslims.

In actual fact, I had always been in touch with the flow of news about what was going on (insert 'in') Iraq. So it wasn't hard for me to comprehend what the woman mentioned. Many things had changed in Iraq after the collapse of Saddam's regime. One of these important things was the ascendance of the Shia Muslim parties to power after the election, which had been held before my trip. This was sufficient to bring changes to all aspects of life.

The gauzy scarf covering her head might be a result of these changes, because she couldn't show her hair under Islamic law (*Sharit*). Anyway, this scarf added a kind of dignity to her appearance, when added to her tidy clothes, as well as introducing the world she lived in. I became sure of this fact when she talked about the purpose of her visit to Amman. She'd had a holiday away from Iraq, although few Iraqi people were able to travel for entertainment because of the hard living conditions in Iraq.

"I got sick of the noise of generators," she mentioned, for most of the Iraqi people had to use generators for producing electric power since the main power supply network hardly functioned.

"Where are you heading for?" she asked me.

"New Baghdad City," I replied, at which her pupils expanded to show much interest.

"That's where I'm going too," she said, while the other passengers began to return back to the car. Soon afterward, we resumed our travel.

We left the 160 Km milepost behind, while the sun was coming up to cover the desert in bright colors. I took off my jacket as the temperature began to rise. I took the notebook out of my jacket pocket, searching for some telephone numbers I had written in it. Without these numbers, I wouldn't be able to reach my family in Baghdad, because they had changed their address years ago. In any case, the most important was my younger sister's phone number. She was living in New Baghdad City, at the south eastern part of Baghdad. She had married my cousin, whom I'd phoned already from Amman, and he had advised me to call him as soon as I arrived in Baghdad.

* * *

We were passing a military barracks, which bordered the road. It was the first sign of the military we'd met since leaving the border. A tank was partly sheltered by embankments of earth, and a soldier could also be seen there, perhaps on duty as a guard. Some civilian features began to appear on the right side of the road. As we descended a hill, a small village came into sight, while we passed many *utes* (utility trucks) carrying containers normally used to store water. It was the first sign of the water shortage that the Iraqi people had been suffering for a long time. For this reason, many drivers were importing these containers from Jordan.

As each kilometer passed, the number of vehicles increased on the road. This increased my sense of security, for I deduced that we were approaching a city. This was confirmed soon when we reached Ramadi, the biggest city of west Iraq.

The city is located on al-Furat River (Euphrates), which partly encircles it before turning to the East. I could see the convoluted river as our car crossed a long bridge leading to the freeway. In this way, we bypassed the city center. I was curious to know what was going on in the city, but after a while, I realized that the driver was right, and I remembered that a huge military action had occurred around this city in early 2004, when the American army attacked Fallujah city, a few kilometers away from Ramadi, to dislodge a radical Islamic group. Since then, Ramadi and Fallujah have become the most rebellious cities in Iraq. They are part of the western Sunni triangle, known as an area of rebellion. This recollection made me understand the strong presence of the American army in this area. Military vehicles of every kind could be seen on the main road, and soldiers were ready for any military action.

As we traveled the last 70 kilometers toward Baghdad, I was able to view many barracks along the main road. I did my best to pinpoint our location but I couldn't, because many things had changed during the twelve years I'd spent out of Iraq.

The tall young man in the middle seat took his mobile phone out of his pocket and began trying to get connected. Despite many tries, he failed because we were a long way from Baghdad. The other passengers also tried frequently to use their mobile phones, but they failed too. Eventually, the woman managed to get connected and started talking with her husband, telling him that she would arrive soon and that she was now in Abu-Ghraib.

Finally, I found myself able to realize where we were— close to the Abu-Ghraib district, about 50 Km west of Baghdad (see p. 180, note #6). This village became very famous because it contains the main prison in Iraq, the "Abu-Ghraib prison," where American correctional officers abused and tortured Iraqi prisoners in 2004.

The tall man also managed to call his family, and after finishing, he turned to me, offering his mobile phone to call my family. Simply, it was a generous offer, and indeed, I needed to make a call. On the other side of the line, there was my sister's voice asking me anxiously where I was calling from. I tried to make it a short call, so I estimated the time needed to arrive in New Baghdad City (New Baghdad is one of nine administrative districts designated as local governmental units after the 2003 invasion; see p. 183, note #1).

"Tell your husband I will meet him in about one hour at the old cinema building in New Baghdad," I told her and ended the call.

The tall man continued his generosity by saying that he intended to rent a taxi as soon as he arrived in Baghdad, and he offered to give me a lift. However, I was too cautious to accept his offer readily. He was still a stranger, in spite of whatever he did for me. Furthermore, his appearance declared that he was a fanatic Muslim. His beard was one of the features that announced this fact, and the ring tone of his mobile phone was from a traditional Muslim song. All these things were enough reasons for me to refuse his offer.

"Thank you, I'll mange it by myself," I said in a polite manner.

"No, it'll be very hard for you to recognize the features of the city after having been away for many years," he said, showing that he was not going to give up easily.

"Don't worry about him; he will come with me; we are going to the same suburb." These winning words came from the lady in the front seat.

"We can share the taxi fare." She turned and talked to me.

The tall man had no comeback in the face of this rescue, and said no more.

Western Baghdad: June 26th, 2005

The traffic became very busy, and then an American military patrol closed the road. Nobody could tell why the road had been closed, but the other passengers guessed that maybe an American patrol had been attacked by the Iraqi insurgents. Nobody in the car showed much attention to what was happening, but they were still watching the traffic, making some comments.

"You'll find such accidents like this every day, welcome back," the ill boy said to me in a joking manner.

Everyone in the car was looking to the left side, where a lot of vehicles formed a long line on a farm beside the main road. All those vehicles turned and left the road, trying to find another way leading into Baghdad.

I was thinking that I had made a mistake in telling my sister that I would meet her husband within an hour, because that one hour had nearly been exhausted, while we were still far away from Baghdad.

Suddenly, our driver turned the car and crossed the

footpath. He made a decision to follow the other vehicles on the unsurfaced, twisting farm path. A ditch divided the farm into two parts, and the vehicles had to drive parallel to the ditch, so that a very long line was formed, and nobody knew if this path would really lead to where we needed to go.

"Have you been along this track before?" I asked the driver.

He laughed and told me it was the first time.

For more than three kilometers, the car snaked along the way, on uneven ground. The potholes made the driving very difficult. I was looking along the ditch, wondering if there was any way that could enable us to cross to the right side.

Eventually, a vaulted bridge appeared along the path and the cars began crossing. On the other side, we were able to see what was happening on the main road we had left. All the passengers in our car turned their faces to look at the other side where an American military vehicle had been attacked and burned in the middle of the road, while many soldiers were moving nervously around[3].

The driver kept following the long line of other cars ahead of us, weaving and crossing an intricate web of country paths among the farms. After about two kilometers, we reached a small village. An asphalt road was in sight now and an Iraqi military patrol had blocked the way, as a checkpoint. The passengers called this patrol the National Guard. They were rather different from the police force. As I found out later, they had some privileges regarding wages and the equipment they were using, and therefore, they were assigned the most dangerous assignments. The new government in Iraq created this kind of force separately from the military or the police, to be ready for any emergency action. Anyway, this checkpoint was very lenient, in that they didn't take more than a few

---

[3] "Suicide bombers hit security forces". *The Telegraph*. 06/27/2005. Page A8, (AP Wire)

moments to release our car.

We had to traverse a short distance before reaching the freeway. Fencing that had once bordered the freeway had long been stolen, so it was easy to get onto the main road without worrying about where the proper on-ramps were.

When the driver reached the freeway, he increased speed as much as he could, trying to cross the distance to Baghdad in a short time. However, after a while, we were caught up in heavy traffic again; the freeway was crowded with cars and the movement nearly ceased, while a police truck was trying to pass through the stopped cars on the opposite side. Some of the policemen were riding in the back, uncovered part of the *ute* and firing in the air. I soon found out that this is frequent: most police in Iraq do this. It must be their way to announce and introduce themselves to the people, but it seemed very rude to me.

I was astonished by all this mess; *things were very much better before I had left Iraq*, I thought. The tall young man got a call from my sister; she'd saved his number when I had called her. She was worried that we were late, while we still struggled to get through to Baghdad city. I told her the reason of our delay, and we revised our arrangements.

Many cars were weaving along the freeway, the drivers searching to find any space to move forward in any direction, without thinking of traffic laws.

After a while, we realized the reason for this chaos: a police checkpoint was blocking the road with many barriers. This made the traffic so heavy. When we approached the checkpoint, the driver seemed very upset and said, "The officer of this checkpoint pushed me to pay fifty thousand Iraqi dinars (about forty dollars) as a bribe three days ago." Meanwhile, the car was rolling through the checkpoint. When the officer waved with his hand to move ahead, the driver took a deep breath. Once beyond the checkpoint, he drove very fast.

* * *

The time was 2:00 pm, and the temperature was gradually rising. We had reached the western part of Baghdad, but I couldn't recognize the area. The reason wasn't only because I had left Baghdad a long time ago, but because I didn't have much information about this region. Dijla River (Tigris) divides Baghdad into two sides. I grew up in the eastern section of Baghdad. However, the western part of Baghdad was the richest, and the most important government offices were located in it.

As we were going across the city, I gradually began to recognize the streets and suburbs. Lots of things had changed, one being the large number of cars in the streets; thousands upon thousands of cars from diverse manufacturers were moving on the busy roads. I never imagined I would see Baghdad so crowded with traffic, but here I was, in the middle of the scene, and I had to accustom my mind to accept this. Apparently, the reason is that after the dramatic changes in the Iraqi regime, the new authority released restrictions on car trade. Cars could be imported without customs duty, and traded without any controls. As a result, most Iraqis had brought cars from outside the country, leading to this mess.

Those passengers who lived in the western part of Baghdad got out. These included the sick boy and the bald man. The car resumed its way, traversing the other part of the city. Wherever we passed, I saw many police vehicles, and as with the first police car we'd seen, policemen were shooting into the air, causing a lot of noise and confusion. They did a lot to worsen the traffic situation.

We were now close to the center of Baghdad. I was surprised, looking at the signs on the walls. It was the first time I saw a sign belonging to the Iraqi Communist Party, since that would have been impossible in Saddam's days.

Crossing to the other side of Baghdad was the hardest due to heavy traffic. We passed behind a building that used to house the Ministry of Information. It looked dusty and abandoned. When the car moved ahead, I looked for the building of the Theater and Cinema Institute, where I used to work as a member of the national theatrical group. But, sadly, the building had entirely burned down, and only the pillars were left. The car crossed the bridge to the other side of Baghdad while I was still looking back to the ruins of the place where I'd spent the most wonderful working times of my life (see p. 180, note #4).

On the other side of the bridge, everything looked different from twelve years before. All the various shops had completely changed. For a long time, these shops had always dealt with agricultural equipment, but now they sold electric generators. Thousands of generators lay on the footpath, and a great many commercial signs covered the fronts of the buildings. I had never seen so many billboards in Baghdad previously, because there had only been a few kinds of national brands allowed. I later found out that all the commercial districts had changed just as radically.

Here we were at al-Sadoon, the main street of Baghdad. It was covered with billboards and signs advertising a great variety of goods. The footpaths were occupied with so many goods that pedestrians had trouble walking along. It wasn't easy for me to apprehend all these changes at once, or to think about them, for the car moved along so quickly.

Eventually, the car stopped at the terminal point at one of the biggest cinema buildings, in al-Sadoon street. I didn't know why the driver chose this place to be the terminal point, but I was able to remember the huge suicide bombings that had occurred a few months before my trip just at this point, where the Baghdad Hotel had been on the other side of the road.

The weather was very hot. This was in June, when the

sun became unbearable after noon, and fortunately, it wasn't hard to find a taxi to drive me with the Christian woman to the suburb of New Baghdad.

The taxi driver gave me an opportunity to tour through the streets that lead to New Baghdad. Many old buildings still stood despite years of war, but now they were covered with dust, and the beautiful clean streets I remembered had become dirty and nauseatingly busy. In New Baghdad, the scene was even worse. I had never seen a mess like this before. The main road was occupied by the vegetable-sellers who had spread out, blocking the way with boxes of vegetables and fruits. The taxi stopped at the old cinema building where I had to get my luggage out and wait to meet Salim.

The old cinema building seemed to be abandoned, and the board used to advertise films was bare and cheerless. The pavement in front of the cinema yard was very dirty and the edge of the sidewalk was broken. Many barriers were put in front of the curbs to prevent cars from stopping nearby, or even to park. I was watching the cars on the street, looking for Salim, thinking it was impossible to expect that he could find a place for parking. Only a few moments later, Salim appeared in his car. He was a rather stout man of about forty-five. His features hadn't changed too much, except that there was grey in his hair, and his front teeth protruded more. We hugged each other and carried the luggage to his old, off-white car.

"I have driven around this place many times, waiting for you to arrive, because I couldn't park anywhere," he said. He explained that any parked car was likely to be suspected, because many cars were used as bombing vehicles, and for this reason, all shopkeepers had put barriers in front of their shops to prevent car parking.

There was no way to avoid the heavy traffic on New-Baghdad's main road, for the barriers on both sides narrowed the road, restricting the passage of the large number of cars. It was almost a shock to look at all these changes on the city, where I had, in fact, spent most of my life.

The sidewalks were completely occupied by the shopkeepers, so that pedestrians had to walk on the road. Many green flags were flapping in the air. These banners were a familiar sign indicating the presence of Shia Muslims everywhere. Thus, it was easy to understand that New Baghdad district had become one of the Shia areas.

Many explosions occurred on the main street of this city, because some radical Sunni groups wanted to kill Shia Muslims. The big roundabout on the main road had been the target of a huge explosion a few months ago when a gas tanker truck exploded among a crowd of poor workers. This had caused a large number of casualties. A lot of people lost their lives, only because they were Shia Muslims.

We were crossing the small bridge to the other side of the water channel that divides New Baghdad into two parts. I recognized the buildings on the other side. I used to live there for some years in a house my father owned. Later, we moved to another suburb. Nothing had changed about these buildings, and they looked as if they had never been touched or renovated since I'd left Iraq. In fact, few of the buildings in the eastern part of Baghdad received any maintenance. The same was true for the streets, sidewalks, roundabouts, and traffic lights. Time had stopped here, and the city was dragging the years of war endlessly. I thought, *How many bombings have these dilapidated buildings borne?* At last, we reached the suburb where my sister lived. Most of the people who lived in that area were teachers, since the government had sold this land to teachers at cheap prices. At any rate, a lot of things had changed during the past years, and many people from different backgrounds had moved into the area; my sister being one of them.

I had also lived in that suburb for many years, because

my father was a teacher as well. Something grabbed my attention at the entrance of the suburb: a great image of one of the Shia leaders was painted on a huge wall, built especially for the image, with some words taken from the Qur'an painted under it. It was clear that the suburb submitted completely to the authority of this Shia leader called "Al-Sader" (full name Mohammad Sadeq Al-Sader). He had been killed in suspicious circumstances during the Saddam days, and his son Muqtada Al-Sader then became the successor to his religious authority.

On the right side of the road, some butchers were slaughtering sheep under the trees and away from any known slaughterhouses. The suburb appeared very tired and dirty, although I did my best to recall the old images from my mind. Eventually I could recognize the markets and the old mosque in the centre of the suburb, and then I was able to arrange the directions and the streets in my memory, while Salim was trying to help me locate the places.

Salim was a successful man, in spite of all the difficulties of living, so he could buy a house, providing a secure life for his family. His work used to be the maintenance of car batteries, a popular career that flourished during war. But like most local industries, his work had become stagnant after the dramatic changes in Iraq. He was now earning his living as a taxi driver. Although his car only had a private license, he used it as a taxi every day, like most Iraqis. People do this without giving any thought to the authorities, which, in any case, aren't concerned about these minor offences.

"This is my house," Salim said as he parked the car over the footpath where there was a black, broad iron gate. When I entered the house, I found my mother and sister waiting anxiously inside. As soon as I arrived, my mother hugged me with tearful eyes, and so did my sister. The first thing I noticed was the wrinkles on my mother's thin face. She looked a lot older than the image I kept in my mind. However, my sister still had the same baby face I loved, but she had put on extra weight. Meeting my family brought a sense of security to me, and all my fears that accompanied me during my trip went away, because I was home.

| **3** | # Home at Last! | |

New Baghdad: June 26th, 2005

It was my first day in my sister's house. Her two children had grown up since I'd left Iraq. The elder one was now a girl of sixteen, and the other, a boy of fourteen. I was so pleased to see them, and they were happy to see me! I could see their pupils dilating as they gazed at me, as if we were meeting for the first time, since they couldn't remember me. I could sense their feeling of excitement at finally standing face to face with their uncle, who lived a million miles away. They probably imagined that I lived in a land of magic, far away from the explosions and the daily bloodshed, where another life could be found.

It was cool inside the house. An air conditioner, powered by a small noisy generator, was working away in the tiny backyard. A few hours later, the rest of my brothers arrived at the house to welcome me. I have three brothers and two sisters, and I am the eldest. The next oldest, Hisham, was forty-seven years old; he was the one who had lost his son. The middle brother, Sami, was in his early forties, and the youngest, Mohamed, was about thirty-five. Time had left its imprint on their features, adding some wrinkles and gray hair. They might have been looking at me and thinking the same thing about my gray hair.

I was still in a state of astonishment because of what I had seen in Baghdad. So when Hisham asked about my opinion of the changes I had seen, I began to talk angrily.

I was sure they couldn't fully appreciate the disaster in which they were living, because they had become accustomed to such scenes over many long years. In a few minutes, the conversation turned to politics and the legality of the American military presence in Iraq.

When Mohamed said it was a Christian war to destroy Islam, the discussion developed spontaneously into a religious debate.

"This is not true, why do you assume that America is the representative of Christianity? This is ridiculous! Can't you see that there are many American Muslim soldiers serving with the troops?" I replied immediately, trying to explain that the Western regimes are run today free from religious influences.

I told him that if George W. Bush wanted to portray himself as a good Christian by attending a church meeting, that didn't make him a representative of the Christians in America, because, after all, a lot of churches had been opposing the invasion of Iraq.

In any case, my comments weren't able to change his opinions, and he still assumed that America's main aim was to destroy Islam, whether in Iraq, Afghanistan, or in any part of the world.

It was easy to see that Mohamed had adopted a radical Islamic perspective, as he made no attempt to hide it behind polite words. He declared openly that everyone who didn't adopt Islam should be treated as an infidel, citing the verse from the Qur'an that reads:

"Everyone who follows a religion other than Islam will be one of the losers."

"But the word 'Islam' in this verse doesn't refer to the religion," I said. "You must read the verses that come before it, to understand the meaning of this verse. The Qur'an says that everyone who submits himself to God is a Muslim," I added, trying to explain the meaning of the complex word-play in that verse.

In fact, most Muslims are confused by this text be-

cause the verb *aslam* in Arabic means: to submit or surrender, and the noun "Muslim" refers to a person who
submits. Thus, everyone who *aslams* himself to God is a
Muslim person, so that the meaning of the verse becomes: everyone who doesn't submit himself to God will
be a loser. By this interpretation, a good Christian or a
good Jew is also a Muslim.

No matter what I said, Mohamed wasn't satisfied with
my interpretation, and neither was Sami, my middle
brother.

I realized that the dispute was becoming more and
more heated, and I didn't want to create an unpleasant
atmosphere between us on my first day back home. So, I
preferred to cease arguing. Besides, I already knew that
arguing with fanatic religious people was useless, since
they can't see past the words of the verses, and, as a result, they won't listen to any opinions opposed to their
beliefs.

In fact, I would not be too surprised if such confront-
ations might have arisen between me and Sami, since I
already knew that he had adopted some sort of Islamic
fundamentalism. But I didn't expect to hear these ideas
from Mohamed, because he had always seemed to have
very little sense of moral responsibility and in his youth
had abandoned his wife and children to go out seeking
pleasure. At any rate, most religious people became fanatical because of serious mistakes they had made in
their past, and it would appear that my youngest brother
was one of those people. But his past still burdened him,
affecting his second marriage, so he now had two wives
and many children; it is normal for Muslims to have more
than one wife.

It was now 6 pm, and Hisham asked me to go back
with him to his home in the adjacent suburb. They were
holding a "consolation meeting" in memory of my brother's son; these are gatherings of relatives held in Arab
countries on the third and the fortieth day after a per-

son's death. I was grateful to my brother for leaving his home, where the consolation meeting was being held, and hurrying over to welcome me.

After leaving my sister's house, Mohamed made his mind up to drive to my brother's place through a popular outdoor market area, thinking it would be a shortcut. Hisham and mother were in the car too, while Sami followed behind in his own car.

In the outdoor markets, there were stalls set up on both sides of the road. Since there was only a narrow gap left, just enough for one car to pass through, our car became stuck when another car came from the opposite direction and blocked the way. Due to the thick crowd of pedestrians, Mohamed couldn't even reverse the car, while the other driver looked completely unperturbed, perhaps secure in his belief that he had the right of way. He was very calm as if time didn't matter to him.

The time we spent waiting gave me an opportunity to look more closely at the shops, which were divided by dirty strips of cloth hung between thin wooden stakes, with some material placed overhead as a shelter from the scorching sun. A terrible stench emanated from the rubbish and spread across the whole area, rendering it unbearable. There were rotting vegetables and the remains of some slaughtered animals lying on the road, attracting flies, while a green Shia flag, which had been set up on one of the shops, was flapping nearby in the breeze.

"What is this? What is the council doing?" I asked resentfully.

"Which council are you talking about? You are in Iraq, not in Australia," Mohamed replied, still trying to reverse out of the traffic jam.

"I can't believe it! A long time has passed since Iraq was liberated and still nobody can fix this mess!"

"Last year was better than this year," commented Hisham. "Every year, things become worse and we sigh for the past year."

"I wish that Saddam, with all his faults, hadn't been deposed," Mohamed said. Nowadays, many Iraqi people believe this.

Eventually, Mohamed managed to find another way forward out of the markets, and I took a deep breath once we were away from the stench. But after a while, I found out that the scene hadn't improved at all. When our car went through the suburb, the streets looked like nobody had cleaned or maintained them in years, and they were covered with putrid water, even though it was June, when it doesn't ever rain in Iraq. I can remember when I was preparing to leave Baghdad in 1994, the initial effects of economic sanctions against Iraq were starting to be obvious, but despite this, the streets were still maintained and in a good condition. Now, they were in a state of disrepair, crowded, and dirty.

On the edge of the suburb, many new houses had been built to form a new area.

The streets of the newly-formed suburb were still not asphalted, so the car was hardly moving. Moreover, piles of construction materials, like bricks, sand, and mesh steel, had been dropped along the edges of the road, almost blocking the way. It was clear that people were gathering without giving any consideration to the council regulations or inspections, which had been very strict during the time of Saddam.

Finally, the car stopped outside a tall iron gate leading into my brother's house. It was a two-storey house but the front part of the top storey was still unfinished.

My niece was the first to come to the door to greet me. I couldn't recognize her at first, for she was now about twenty years old. She wore a long black dress, as did all the women inside the house.

It was clear that the consolation meeting in this house was held only for women, and some close male relatives. I passed by the faces of many women. Some of them greeted me, while others kept looking at my features and whispering, trying to recall my face.

I went into the back room with my brothers. There were many women I didn't recognize. The exception was Nawal, one of my cousins. This woman might have become my wife once. We were brought up together, so we were very close friends and all our relatives thought we would be a good match for each other, regardless of the fact that I had always looked upon her as my sister. A long time had passed since the last time we'd seen each other, but she hadn't changed a lot, and her baby face still reminded me of the young girl with whom I had built a chicken coop in our old backyard.

I was sitting beside her husband and talking about how my nephew had lost his life so early. But although he was very close to me, he didn't recognize me, or maybe he was pretending. Anyhow, I'd never liked him, ever since the first day I met him. If I'd had a choice, I wouldn't have approached him, not only because of his huge body size, but also because holding a high rank in the army had roughened his character as happened to most military officers in Saddam's regime. While the other room was occupied exclusively by women, our room was not. It was in fact my brother's bedroom, and the double bed took up most of the space. A tall slim man, about forty years old, was sitting on the edge of it, telling the tragic story of my nephew.

I was concentrating hard, trying to understand all the details of the accident.

My nephew had got a job as a bodyguard to Fawaz al-Jarba, a senior parliament member in Mosul, a city in the north of Iraq (Nineveh). The fatal accident occurred when a gang of insurgents had attacked the parliament member's residence and surrounded it. My nephew was one of ten guards who were defending the house. The parliament member had called in the American forces to rescue him, but by the time they arrived, the gangs had already retreated.

Unfortunately, the American forces led by the 3rd Battalion, 21st Infantry Regiment, attacked the house anyway, thinking that the terrorists had taken control of it, and this misunderstanding led them to kill all of the security guards, except the man who was telling the story, who had been the team's leader.[4]

The people in the room tried to show their concern and sadness; but whatever they felt, it couldn't compare with the depth of the grief of the victim's parents, especially his mother's.

My nephew Yaseer Hisham was a young boy of about twenty-two years. He got married early after falling in love with the neighbor's daughter. That girl had now become a widow when she was only three months pregnant.

The young man who told the story was still sitting on the edge of the bed.

He must be one of the relatives of my brother's wife, I thought to myself, because he was behaving quite frankly. Suddenly, Hisham's wife rushed into the room and grabbed hold of the man.

"Why were you saved while my son had been killed? Why?" she screamed angrily.

"You should have protected him; you offered him this job; and he was in your responsibility!" she added, while some women tried to pull her off the man.

"I couldn't do anything. We were hiding in a bathroom when the Americans broke into the place, and threw a hand grenade... how could we have avoided a grenade?" the man defended himself.

"So why did the bomb miss you but not my son? Why?" she sobbed, with eyes full of tears, while the others tried to pacify her that it was fate and no one could have changed it. Most of the Iraqi people surrender themselves completely to fate, as it is the only thing that can

---

[4] "Politician: U.S. Troops Caused Some Casualties", *USA Today*, May 19th, 2005. Mona Mahmoud and Steve Komarow.

simply explain what is happening around them, and why all these casualties are occurring, every day.

As it seemed to do on every occasion where people gathered and talked together, the discussion soon turned to political affairs, and in no time to the American occupation of Iraq.

All the comments were filled with frustration, as people found that their lives had become worse than they had been under Saddam's regime. Also, the American soldiers had begun to deal with the people very roughly and cruelly after the heavy resistance from the Sunni insurgents, especially as the number of American causalities continued to mount day after day. I didn't yet fully appreciate how the Americans were dealing with people, because the only image I had in my mind of the Americans, at that point, was what had happened to me at the border. But day by day, I came to realize how the American occupation of Iraq was terrifying people, as I saw the fear that was clearly visible on their faces while they drove along the streets, being careful to give way to the American military vehicles.

My mother told me later about one of my cousins who had been killed by an American military vehicle when she was driving with her husband one afternoon, last Ramadan, the Muslim holy month. She hadn't noticed the cautionary waving of the soldier on the fast American military vehicle behind her. So she failed to give way, which provoked the military vehicle to smash into the back of her car, and she was killed as the force of the impact overturned the car.

My family still believed it was my cousin's fate that she would die that way, even if she had taken every possible precaution. A similar philosophy inspired the great writers of Greek tragedies, such as Sophocles, who told how the King Oedipus tried in every possible way to avoid killing his father and marrying his mother, but was unable to escape the fulfillment of the prophecy made at his birth.

Destiny and fate are foundational principles in a Muslim's beliefs, with many Qur'anic verses confirming their importance.

And so, as she tried to console my nephew's grieving mother, my cousin Nawal said, "It was his fate to die at that moment in that place."

Behind their expressions of sympathy, however, I could sense that all the eyes in the room were gazing accusingly at my brother Hisham and his wife, blaming them for pressuring their son to take such a risky job.

In a few seconds, the conversation moved on to a discussion of Al-Jehad, which refers to the duty of Muslims to fight and defend their religion against the enemy.

"He died as a martyr. Anybody killed by the Americans becomes a martyr," said Nawal, and the others agreed with her. It seemed that she now led the conversation. This surprised me at first, but soon afterward, I found out that she had graduated from a religious college (al-Shariat) and had become the family counselor, to whom people turned whenever there was a disagreement about religious topics.

"What does Shariat (Islamic law) say about a Muslim if he plans to leave Iraq during these hard times, to seek a more secure life?" my brother Sami asked her, because he was considering doing just that himself.

"Deserting Iraq at this time is a sort of dereliction of duty in Al-Jehad, because it is the Muslim's duty to fight against Islam's enemies at this critical time," she asserted unhesitatingly. Meanwhile, my brother Hisham leaned over and whispered to me that she had banned her husband from leaving the house, because she was afraid that his life might be endangered.

"According to the Qur'an, Islam encourages a Muslim to fight in defense of his property, his women, his religion. So if anybody dies defending these things, he will be a martyr."

She continued preaching while the others listened carefully.

"What do you think about the suicide bombings, which target the American forces but kill a lot of innocent people by mistake" I asked deliberately.

"Well... the innocent people who might have been killed by mistake, they became martyrs," she answered.

"I don't care whether they become martyrs or not. I am asking why they lose their lives. Who is responsible? Is it the Americans or the fighters?"

"The Americans are responsible, definitely, because they occupied the country," she replied confidently.

"But that's not fair. It's the fighters who killed them, not the Americans."

"Are you opposing fighting the Americans!? So how will we drive them out of Iraq then?" Sami interjected.

"There must be many things we can do; fighting is not the only way. You can see that fighting the Americans has only worsened the situation, by adding more bloodshed every day," I argued. The faces around me were regarding me more suspiciously, and nobody tried to take the argument any further. Even though Nawal began to choose some quotation from the Qur'an, they were unrelated, so I realized she was trying to change the subject, because her movements, her features, and the tremor in her voice all showed her deep embarrassment. In the end, she left the room pretending to clear a small table, taking the empty glasses out of the room.

* * *

Some visitors had left the consolation meeting, creating a little space in the crowded house. My mother invited me into the other room, which many women had already left, so that only the close relations remained. When I entered the room, Hisham's wife was sitting motionless, and grief covered her face like the black suit which covered her body. Now that she had calmed down, I could talk to her, and express my sympathy.

The room was narrow and long; only a few women were enough to fill it. A large photograph of a young boy, marked with a black stripe, was hanging on the wall. I could tell that it must be my nephew's photo despite not having seen him for the past twelve years. The details of his face had completely changed, and the little boy had grown up into a handsome young man with blue eyes.

"Look at his face; look how good-looking he was! Have you met his wife?" Hisham's wife said, breaking the silence, as she pointed to a young girl, about seventeen years old, who was squatting on the ground.

"She's three months pregnant," she added.

I wondered to myself what kind of life this young widow could have, after losing her husband less than a year into their marriage. I asked myself what she was going to do with her child. Truly, I found this widow's situation more tragic than the story of my nephew, since his life had finished but she was still living, and she would suffer and struggle alone without any kind of social security or insurance. She might not be thinking too much about her future now, because she was only seventeen, but she would find out the miserable reality of her life sooner or later.

Many relatives had to stay in my brother's house since they had come from Mosul (Nineveh), one of the largest cities to the North (see p. 186, note #2). Hence, I didn't want to be a burden, preferring to stay in my sister's house, despite the insistence of my brother and his wife to stay for the night with them. Another reason I preferred my sister's house was that it was so quiet.

| 4 | **Coping with Life in Baghdad** |  |

New Baghdad: June 27th, 2005

I got up rather late the day after that long, dangerous, grueling trip. The sound of the TV woke me up; otherwise, I would have slept even longer. It was the morning news bulletin, and I saw that many explosions had occurred yesterday in Baghdad. One of these had been in front of the old Al-Bayda cinema building in New Baghdad City, the same place where I had waited for Salim upon my arrival in New Baghdad[5]. The explosion had occurred at 4 p.m. and I might have been one of those casualties if I had been there only two hours later.

I started the day with a traditional Iraqi breakfast, like most families in Baghdad. It consists of thick buffalo cream with hot fresh bread and tea. The cream is made by village people using a traditional method, without any regard for modern health and hygiene standards. However, I couldn't resist the delicious taste of that morning meal, which I always used to have in the past. Earlier that morning, my mother had asked Salim to buy it, because she knew how much I liked it.

Actually, this meal was and still is an important part of the traditional Baghdadi culture, with most people buying the cream and bread fresh every morning. Normally, people purchase it from the farming women who come in from the adjacent villages before sunrise to sell their merchandise, either directly to the people, or to the shops. It

---

[5] "Four wounded in east Baghdad car blast." *Al-Sharqiyah*, Baghdad. 06/27/2005.

is one of the familiar sights of Baghdad: people holding out their plates to the village women who sit by the road, with their merchandise on a broad metal plate, covered with a plain sheet of paper or fabric.

After breakfast, I wanted to go out into the front yard. Despite the fact that it was summer, the air outside was still cool for the first part of the day, because the front yard was shaded by a Lote-tree belonging to the neighbor's house, spreading over the brick fence, creating a wide shady area. Most households in Iraq consider this tree to be blessed because it is mentioned in the Qur'an, and most people believe that they shouldn't cut it down. I hadn't seen this tree since I left Iraq. Even in Jordan, where I had lived for many years, it wasn't available, although Jordan is adjacent to Iraq.

While I sat in the shade of the branches bending over the fence, a stream of sentiments burst forth from my soul, carrying with them many happy childhood memories of climbing up to the highest branches and plucking the small round fruits.

I sat on a wooden bench in the front yard, thinking about my trip to Iraq. It was unbelievable; being in my sister's home was like being in a dream, because I'd never thought it could ever become a reality.

I'd left Iraq in 1994 to work in Jordan for the Al-Moustakbale (literally, "The Future") radio station belonging to the Al-Wifaq Iraqi National Accord, one of the Iraqi opposition groups. I used to dream about returning home, but every morning I'd wake, still an exile, because I had opposed Saddam's regime and he had a lasting memory.

I tried to show no fear for my life, but despite all efforts, fear came up eventually when my homesick dreams transformed into nightmares.

Abruptly, I'd find myself in the main bus station in Central Baghdad, and the awe began when I grew conscious that I was working in a radio station against

Saddam's regime. Among the huddle of folks, I was not able to identify any one person. I desperately strived to get out lest someone recognize me, but to no avail. I struggled mightily through a never-ending mass of people until I woke up sweat-drenched.

Frequently, this nightmare altered, taking different variations. I'd find myself suddenly popped up from an unreal realm to one of the places in Iraq which lay deep in my unconscious. For instance, the office where I had been recruited for the compulsory military service in Baghdad; and like before, I'd realize how immense a mistake I had made by venturing to come to Baghdad while still opposing Saddam. Though it was a nightmare, it also was funny because, within it, I was preoccupied with getting my salary from the radio station and how I could receive it while being in Iraq.

Nightmares may have reflected the perilous times I'd spent in Jordan, contending against one of the most authoritative regimes in modern history. Confronting Saddam was not trouble-free even in Jordan, for he had a great intelligence service around the world using the enormous amount of resources in Iraq that enabled him to recruit whoever, whenever, and wherever he wanted.

In Jordan, the grounds were favorable for the Iraqi intelligence agents to work effectively, not only because Jordan is adjacent to Iraq, but also owing to the great advocates of Saddam within it. We had to anticipate that problems could have happened at any time, but we did not expect that risks were so very close. Much later, we found out that Iraqi intelligence had even planted spies among us. We were stunned to know that everything was exposed to Iraqi intelligence and they had kept a close watch on our work in the radio station, as well as our personal lives, which increased our apprehensions and we grew aware that we were facing a giant opponent.

The Iraqi intelligence service kept using this information to terrify us as much as they could. By ordered plan, they began to send messages to some of our members using different ways; they used to tell them, for instance, that they already knew everything about their lives, using threats to get them to resign from the radio station, or to become part of their system by employing them as a double-agent. As for me, I used to receive some short calls from an unknown person, attempting to terrify me. Consequently, I had to change my lodging and telephone number many times.

Like my workmates, I believed that the Iraqi authorities could have finished us very easily, but maybe they were following the proverb: "Strike down the shepherd, and the sheep will be scattered." As a result, there was a high level of security provided by Jordanian intelligence to the opposition's leadership. Five years had passed at the radio station, with no way to know who those spies were. And this amplified our suspicion, distrust, and wariness.

* * *

My mother appeared in the front yard to ask me to visit one of my cousins, Yousef, who lived nearby. Yousef was still traumatized by a horrible experience that had happened weeks ago: being part of a group of people who had been kidnapped by terrorists.

His job as a van driver exposed him to these sorts of risks, and my mother explained what had happened to him. A group of passengers hired two vans, including his, to take them to Hussaiba, a small town in the western part of Iraq. They found themselves at a roadblock just a few kilometers short of their destination, where armed men forced them out. Most of the passengers were killed just because they were Shia Muslims. The terrorists had recognized their denomination from their names, which were displayed on identification papers. The passengers and the other driver were slain, but Yousef was held captive for a week, and then released, just because he had a Sunni name. This horrible experience left Yousef traumatized for a week before he regained some of his psychological balance.

As Yousef lived close by, Salim gave my mother and me a lift, before beginning his morning's work as a taxi driver. Yousef's house has a long front yard, so that if anyone knocks at the main gate, he may have to wait for long time before someone comes to open the gate. Most Iraqi people have forgotten about using electric bells for they are always out of order due to poor electricity supply and fluctuation.

Finally, someone heard the knocks and the door opened. It was Yousef who hurried to open the main gate and receive us. He looked perplexed and confused, as he asked us in a low voice to keep silent about whatever we heard inside his home. In a few words, he explained that his family was out, and the parents of the other driver, who had been killed in Hussaiba, were visiting to inquire about their son. When we got inside the small old house, there were two men and a woman. One of the men seemed to be a Sunni preacher. He was a huge, bulky old man with a long grey beard. The other man and the woman sounded like southern villagers. The room was too narrow and there was no available space to add more chairs, but we were able to find a place to sit down and listen to these people.

While we were listening to the conversation, we realized that Yousef wasn't telling them the whole truth. He attempted to hide their son's fate from them. For this reason, he was talking around the point, trying to avoid telling them the complete truth. I could see many questions written on their faces, and they were anxiously trying to catch any hint that might lead them to important information. The visitors asserted that they had gone to the place of the crime, but they hadn't been able to get any evidence proving the death of their son.

It wasn't the first time these people had visited Yousef's house. They had been here a week ago, when Yousef had revealed to them some facts, but not all. The mother was the most anxious to get Yousef shed some more light on the disappearance of her son. I could see her eyes begging for any useful details as she asked Yousef over and over again to tell her frankly whether her son had been killed or had survived. However, Yousef persisted in reiterating what he had said before, telling them that the terrorists had blindfolded him, and taken him away to another place, where he was held for a week, stating that that was the reason why he couldn't know what had happened to their son.

However, the parents didn't give up and they kept questioning. Even when they were about to leave, they asked Yousef to allow them to visit him again, although he insisted that he didn't have any thing to add.

Despite all their questions about every tiny detail, there was still one important question, as evident from their features, one they couldn't ask: "Why did the terrorists release you but not our son? And was that because you are a Sunni while our son is a Shia?"

I could sense they might have wished to ask this, but they didn't, maybe because they felt that it would be improper. Yousef sensed this too and he revealed his thoughts to me after they had left.

"The man with the long beard was brought to encourage me to tell the truth because he is a Sunni preacher," Yousef said.

"They might have thought he would be able to persuade me to talk, but I just want to put the whole thing behind me. In any case, if I told them the truth, they might accuse me of cooperating with the terrorists."

After they had left, Yousef suggested we visit his mother, who lived in the same neighborhood, just to get away from the gloomy atmosphere of the house. We used his van to get to his mother's house, but, first of all, he wanted to show us the new house he was constructing. It was an unfinished building just across the street, a few hundred meters away.

The land where he was building had been a military camp in Saddam's time, but the local agent of the Shia religious leader Muqtada Al-Sader had conquered the land and sold it to the people at a low price. It was an illegal deal, and the dwellers didn't have any documents to prove their ownership, except the contract they had signed with the agent of Muqtada Al-Sader. Thousands of houses had been constructed without any planning or government approval, but only via the authorization of a powerful religious leader who did not even own the land. However, Yousef was optimistic about the future, and he expected that the government would empathize with them and recognize their ownership; but until that time, they wouldn't be able to connect to the electricity grid, the network of water pipes, or the sewage system.

"In any case, I don't expect the government will be able to supply all these services for ten years!" Yousef said while he was driving from his incomplete house to his mother's dwelling place.

Small and simple, that was my aunt's one-bedroom home. She lived alone, as all her sons and daughters had moved out. This woman, who had always been so strong, had become unable to straighten up, and her eyesight had weakened so much that she couldn't recognize me when I entered her home. I wondered how she was managing by herself. It is a very sad experience to see people at the end of their lives without any programs or government plans to support and care for them.

* * *

Visiting my cousin Yousef opened my eyes to what was going around me. What I had heard and seen was not fiction, but real tragedy. I could read its pages when I was looking at the victim's mother; it was the early sign of a brewing civil war. My arguments with my brother Mohamed over the next few days confirmed my fears, because he was always verbally attacking the Shia Muslims, calling them infidels and saying that they should be punished under Islamic law. He even refused to shop at any butcher from a Shia background, believing that the meat they sell is not *halal* (permissible by Islamic law). I always objected by saying, "We shouldn't judge people for their religious opinions, even if they seem faulty; only God has the right to judge people." At any rate, my arguments weren't able to persuade Mohamed, who always relied on a religious text to support him. In this text, the Prophet Mohammed calls upon Muslims to use force to change anything that is contrary to Islamic law. Most radical Muslims base the legitimacy of what they do on an interpretation of this text as a call for violent action.

A new state of affairs was beginning to take shape among the ruins, where the relationship between the Sunni and Shia Muslims had been broken. This relationship couldn't be fixed by the political propaganda that declared reconciliation every day between all denominations in Iraq. The Iraqi society, indeed, had always been tolerant of the religious differences between the Sunni and Shia Muslims, but it seemed that the long honeymoon was now approaching its end. The denominational differences were regaining their old potency, just like they had when the conflict first broke out between the Muslim leaders, after the death of Prophet Mohammed, about who was capable of succeeding him.

New Baghdad: June 30th, 2005

Life in my sister's house followed a particular routine. Since there was only one air conditioner, there was only one part of the house in which the family could find shelter from the summer heat, and everyone had to crowd in. The house consisted of two rooms, a bathroom and a kitchen, with a small living area in the centre. The upper rooms were rented out to another family and could only be entered via an external stairway. All the land had once been part of their neighbor's large garden.

A lot of property-owners in Baghdad had had to sell half of their properties, or divide their houses into two parts, in order to get some relief from the crushing financial burdens. The six or seven hundred square meters of patches of land on which people used to build their houses had been shrunk gradually year after year, and they could not be found easily nowadays in these suburbs.

We all slept in the living area, arranging all our single mattresses as best as we could in the limited floor-space. Although it was inconvenient, it increased the sense of intimacy. It reminded me of the early days of my childhood, when all the children in the house were crammed on one mattress, playing gaily; we lost this sense once we grew up and dispersed to look for our individuality.

Lying on the floor and watching some satellite TV programs, when all the lights in the house had been turned off (so we would have enough electricity to power both the air conditioner and TV), gave us a lot of pleasure during those long summer nights.

All Iraqi people enjoy watching satellite television, which had all been prohibited under Saddam's regime. During the period I had lived in Jordan, I would hear some spreading news from Baghdad telling that Saddam was trying to provide some of these satellite channels to be watched publicly in Iraq. Attempting to circumvent free broadcasting, he kept planning to avert direct transmission by recording some programs from these channels and re-transmitting them. He was not able to listen to any voice opposed to him.

But now, we had many favorite programs that we watched regularly, and the best was a new independent Iraqi channel (Al-Sharkia), whose broadcasts were frank and free from government control.

At night, Salim was ever only half-asleep, because he had to turn the generator on or off, according to the availability of electric power. He had installed a switch for moving from the generator to the main power grid. Most families use this method, but some of them have larger-sized generators, and so are able to use many rooms, each of them having its own air conditioner. Other families pay a monthly fee to the owners of large industrial generators, who usually set them up on the sidewalks of some streets, supplying houses with electric power using external wires.

As for fresh water, and because the municipal water pumps were not powerful, private water pumps were placed permanently on the pipelines of all houses to pump up water. Salim used to spend a lot of time every day setting up the water pump, as it should be emptied of air before being able to suck up water and pump it to the spare water tank; and if he could not cope with this work, we would not have been able to have a bath, and also had to be quite conservative in using water on that day. However, even with private water pumps, it would not have been possible, for there was often a shortage of water in the water mains.

When my sister came to ask how it was going, Salim turned off the water pump.

"It does not work; no bath today," said Salim in vain.

"Ok, leave it; I only want to remind you that the coming days will be the time to fetch our food ration," she said, but Salim belittled this matter; he murmured some words, deprecating the food ration. He was financially independent, so he wouldn't have to rely on these subsidized food rations.

These rations had been issued in Saddam's days when Iraq was under economic sanctions. The Iraqi government after 2003 still depended on these coupons as they became a reliable proof for identity and address, maybe much more than personal ID cards.

My memory is still vivid in recalling the hard times I had lived in Iraq when I had to yield to the monthly suffering of getting these subsidized food rations from "agent shops", small grocery stores present in all Iraqi cities. The terribly long queues and the noisy complaints of people about the items' weight, all these scenes came alive to my mind in a second. How humiliating it was to live hard like that for a monthly ration consisted of a few kilograms of rice, sugar, flour, and a liter of cooking oil.

"It shrinks every year; now we are lucky if we get a few kilograms of flour. Last month we could only get a couple of handfuls of rice and a single soap," Salim said scoffingly while he got in the house.

Being in Bagdad again, after having been away from my family for long years, was a reason to bring my brothers to my sister's home every evening. Another reason was that my mother used to spend most of her time in this home. Although she owned a small apartment in south-eastern Baghdad, she still preferred to live with my sister for several reasons. All the family members lived in New Baghdad suburbs, except my elder sister, so she could be close to them. Besides, it was a quiet home, and also because Salim was a kinsman. Mother tried to buy another apartment in New-Baghdad but the prices were out of reach. As she became older, she grew more sensitive and had a delicate temperament. Any trivial problem used to drive her to disturbance, and she would say in a loud voice "I need to go home; I am not comfortable away from it." But after one day away from my sister's home, she would return saying that it was tedious to be alone. To fill the gap left by my father's departure, long years ago, she would move from one home to another, choosing my sister's home as a main meeting place. She managed to scrape by with an adequate living, depending on a meager pensioner salary as well as the crumbs of money given to her by my brothers and sisters.

In the evening, when all the brothers gathered, there were many topics to talk about. But the most interesting issue to them was the Muslim culture in Australia. I used to tell them how Muslims live in Australia and how they still maintained their own traditions and conventions despite living in a different culture. However, as much as I told them, they were not able to conceive the shape of life in Australia and its images would elude them.

Being an Australian citizen, they thought I would be able to facilitate immigration procedures for them. In fact, Sami was the most concerned about this issue while the others used to inquire mainly out of curiosity.

As a matter of fact, concerns about religious life struck me as soon as I had arrived in Iraq. When I left Iraq in 1994, none of my family even knew how to pray as seasoned Muslims, but now I felt as if I was dwelling in a mosque. When the time was due for Muslim prayer, everyone in my sister's home turned their bodies in the direction of Mecca to pray. Even the children got used to practicing Islamic life; the boys would go frequently to the mosques with their fathers, as every practicing Muslim did on Friday, and the girls used to wear scarves, praying behind men in the home.

I still remembered that my father, when he became older, turned to religion and prayed regularly. He did these sorts of practices as heavy obligations, never knowing if God would accept his prayers, or even to be sure if God was real or fictitious.

Not only my family was caught up in religious zest, but most Iraqi people I met were too, especially the people from Sunni society.

In most cases, people turn to religion when they become weighed down with heavy burdens that they can no longer endure. On the same premise, the long suffering of the Iraqi people compelled them to grapple with religion after they had found that their catastrophes were everlasting. They had spent eight years in a war with Iran, followed by the invasion of Kuwait, and endured for thirteen years resisting the consequences of the economic sanctions inflicted by the U.N. in 1990 as a result of this adventure. And finally came the invasion of Iraq and whatever ensued; all these things left their mark on social life.

5	**Overcoming My Fears**	

New Baghdad: July 6th, 2005

I was very cautious during the first days after my arrival, and my movements were very limited. But after that I began to go with my brother Sami, every morning, to his garage, which was about two kilometers from my sister's house. Sami would pick me up every morning in his car and I'd spend most of the day with him.

I was very careful about wandering outside alone in the beginning, but, over time, I began to become desensitized to the dangers, so I was able to get around by myself using public transport. This consisted of minivans driven by private citizens. I preferred this kind of transportation to the small taxies because I thought that being with other people in a vehicle might reduce the risks to safety. Of course, I knew that this was a false sense of security because once you go outside the house or on the road, the potential for danger is increased, no matter what precautions are taken.

In fact, the roads are the most dangerous places in Baghdad, especially when there is an American military force around, because nothing terrifies people as much as the American military. There is always a sign on the back of the military vehicles warning any cars not to approach closer than three hundred meters and in some cases, five hundred meters. However, cars always kept more than five hundred meters away or maybe a thousand meters, to avoid any trouble.

* * *

On Channel Street, which divides New Baghdad city into two, there was always a strong American military
presence (see p. 182, note #2). As Sami's garage faced directly onto the Channel Street, I was able to watch the
military vehicles going past all day. I could expect to see
some military vehicles passing every ten minutes or less.
At first, I couldn't understand the reason for that heavy
presence in this area, but in time, I learned that the
American military had established two camps near
Channel Street. The first was located at the end of Channel Street, about two kilometers away from the garage.
This had once been the location of the academy for the
military officers of the previous Iraqi regime. The other
camp was much closer to the garage; it had been established on the site of the old Department of Internal
Security building of Saddam's regime.

Many rumors had spread about these camps, telling of
prostitutes being brought every day to provide pleasure to
the American soldiers, but there was no way to verify
these rumors. At any rate, whether true or false, these
rumors had a very negative impact because the Iraqi
community is extremely conservative.

Since these camps were inside the city, the American
military tanks were always demolishing the streets, leaving behind a lot of ruin, without any consideration for the
city's inhabitants. Because Channel Street leads to the
southern cities of Iraq, I used to see a lot of military tanks
passing by on that street in Saddam's days, but these
tanks were carried on trailers in order to keep the streets
from being damaged.

* * *

The first time I went to Sami's garage by myself, I was
able to conquer my fears, venturing out and strolling on
Baghdad's streets alone without looking for somebody to
escort me. The driver of the public van I rode dropped me
off in Channel Street, and then I had to cross the two
busy main streets, which run parallel to both sides of the

channel, before reaching the garage.

Most of my youth had been spent in this area and it had been one of the favorite places for spending nights with friends. Along this channel, many open-air bars would stay open long past midnight. As my parents' house was just across the street, I used to waste long hours drinking beer and having fun with my friends.

However, all these scenes had disappeared and gone with the wind, and a new reality faced me as I was crossing the Channel by a footbridge, because putrid water had stagnated, polluting the area. I crossed the footbridge in a hurry to get away from the stench.

My brother's garage was quite small, and it dealt only with wrecked German cars. Because his previous career had come to a stop, Sami had established this new business as an auto-wrecker. He had worked in liquid battery manufacturing for many years and he had achieved success in that field, but the unstable circumstances in Iraq had affected his business. After the breakdown of the previous regime, the borders of Iraq had been opened wide to foreign imports, causing a great deal of harm to local manufacturers.

When I walked in, Sami was involved in dealing with one of his customers as usual. I took a seat in the front yard, looking through the iron bars of the fence at Channel Street. I was pleased to look at the cars, trees, and people, in spite of all the ruin around me. Something in my soul was attracted to everything, even though it was in such a mess.

The palm trees along the channel street looked sad and were dull-colored. The dust covered everything, the streets, the houses, and even the sky lost its brightness. Were they the same scenes I had known before or might they have been beautified by my memories?

* * *

The garage was a place where some of Sami's friends met and chatted about different aspects of life. The most interest was generated by discussions over the existence of the American troops in Iraq, looking for a way to emigrate from Iraq, and Islamic topics. Regarding the first issue, according to all the people I had met, no one was happy with the invasion of Iraq because they found out, at last, that their life had become much worse than before. The conversation would start with remembering the old days when they had never suffered lack of electricity, serious shortage of fresh water, sewage problems, and very poor security. Then the talks drifted away to scan the incidents that had occurred during the past twenty-four hours, and the American military vehicles which had been attacked by the al-Mujahideen (which means the Islamic fighters). No one ever called them terrorists in Iraq, except for the official media. However, the conversation did not lack overstatement, in that some of Sami's friends exaggerated the number of American casualties while minimizing those of the fallen Islamic fighters.

As for emigrating from Iraq, it was and still is the dream for everyone, even children. It was an opportunity to some of Sami's friends to ask me about the probabilities of getting a chance to immigrate to Australia, and I was patient to answer all their questions because they wanted me to be very accurate and precise. They always looked at me as if I had come from a different planet; I tried with great effort to explain the shape of life overseas, but they were not able to imagine it because none of them had ever left Iraq. When the subject changed to Islamic topics, they would pay careful attention and show enthusiasm. I did not want to interfere in these subjects, knowing how sensitive they were. But sometimes, things drifted away unexpectedly, and in less than a moment, everything was out of control.

It was afternoon, and as frequently, Sami and two of his friends asked me about the life in Australia and the government unemployment payments, which was a profound act and beyond their understanding. They were sitting in a circle outside of the small office room where some chairs were placed in a shady spot. Despite the fact that he did not comprehend the system of social security in the western regimes, Sami commented that this rule had been borrowed from Islam and they all agreed with him. Though I would have liked to challenge this, I preferred to remain quiet.

When the conversation turned to matrimony, one of the customers intruded to give his notion. Owing to his point of view on temporary matrimony, which is permitted only in Shia Islamic law, it seemed evident that he was a Shia Muslim. Although all the listeners were Sunni orthodox Muslims, no one raised an objection or commented upon this opinion which tossed a disputed issue between Shia and Sunni Muslims. Sami tried to conceal his anger but his eyes were glowing with irritation. The silence encouraged the customer to expound on his idea, showing the necessity of the temporary matrimony by saying that when Muslim men went to war, or on a long trip, they could make an agreement with a woman to marry her for a short term. The discussion developed to discuss one of Prophet Mohammed's raids against the Jews of Khyber, a tribe which used to live in Arabia in the sixth century A.D., and the story of Safia, the daughter of the Jew's king.

The story tells that the Muslim fighters had besieged the fortress of the Jews for a long time, and finally broken in. As a result, Prophet Mohammed had married the daughter of the Jewish king at the same day her father, husband, and all her male relatives had been killed.

The Islamic references tell us that Mohammed gave Safia the choice to live with Muslims after converting to Islam or to stay as a Jew with her tribe, and she chose to convert to Islam. They were appreciating the attitude that was taken by this woman when she chose to stay with the Muslim side, despite her ordeal. When the customer nodded to me for approval, I said tepidly:

"Well, I've read this story before, but even if the histori-cal references were true, I can't understand how she could be happy in this marriage!"

It was clear that my interference did not please them, as they still silently stared me. While the silence grew op-pressive, an admonishing inner voice cautioned me to wisdom, but I realized that there was no way to retreat and I might as well go on to the end of the discussion.

"She was happy, she converted to Islam, and accepted to be a wife to Prophet Mohammed by her will," Sami said assertively.

"Are you trying to persuade me that this woman was happy in this marriage despite the fact that her father, husband, and male relatives had all been killed in one day?" I did all my best to emphasize that after the battle, all the Jewish women had become captives, and this woman was one of them, according to the Islamic histori-cal references, but he refused to believe, persisting that she wasn't a captive.

"If you read the history, you will find that Prophet Mo-hammed set her free after he married her." I tried to explain this fact while he kept persisting.

"She wasn't a captive, she was free when she converted and married, because she believed in Islam, and don't tell me about her family members who were all killed, be-cause God could change her heart to Islam whatever she suffered." That was the last word he said, because then I preferred to keep silent, seeing that the discussion was useless.

A coincidence occurred that evening. We were at my sister's home as usual, when an Islamic program was running on one of the TV channels, talking about the same battle. The message of the preacher on TV was very clear when he said that some Muslim fighters had asked Prophet Mohammed after the battle if they could keep the Jewish women as part of the spoils and Mohammad had permitted taking them because they were captives as Mohammed had said.

I think luck was on my side: Sami was carefully watching that program.

"Didn't you hear? They were captives. He is a Muslim preacher who talks, don't argue with me!" I exclaimed while he kept silent. But after a while, he burst out in anger, accusing me of disparaging the sanctity of Prophet Mohammed.

"I didn't, I only tried to analyze the attitude of this woman. I consider that she converted to Islam because she was afraid of being killed. Can't you see I am merely trying to use my mind?" I asked emphatically, concluding the discussion.

I was sure that what happened that afternoon wasn't by accident and that God was revealing the truth to my brother, but he was unable to accept it as the voice of God. He might have accepted this historical fact if it had come from someone else, but he built high walls between us because I had chosen Christianity instead of Islam. He did not confront me or ask me obviously about my faith, but almost certainly, he had been told by my mother as she was already acquainted with my conversion while she had called in to see me in Jordan in 2000.

In any case, my relationship with Sami was fractured for the next few days until he approached me, trying to fix what had been broken, and so I forgave him for his anger. But he kept seizing any opportunity to drag me into arguments about Islam and I was finally able to understand that he was trying to convert me to Islam.

I tried many times to avoid these anticipated discussions because they were futile, and as well, such arguments would have agitated anyone having religious sensibility. I knew that each of us had chosen our own way and there was no way to find a junction. He was a fanatic Muslim, while I converted to Christianity many years ago, and my faith and loyalty were toward Jesus Christ.

New Baghdad: July 13th, 2005

Going to the garage during the first two weeks of my arrival in Baghdad gave me the opportunity to meet some of my relatives, whom I had lost contact with over the past twelve years. They used to come to obtain spare parts for their cars, or to ask my brother to give them a hand because he was a trained mechanic. One of my cousins whom I met like this had been a pilot in Saddam's army, but now he had become one of the thousands of unemployed Iraqis who had lost their jobs due to a decision of Paul Bremer, the former civilian governor of Iraq, to demobilize all members of the former Iraqi army.

I could only talk with this cousin for a short time, since he was in a hurry to look for a new home for his family after the serious warning he'd received from a staunch friend who told him that Al-Mahdi Shia militia listed his name in its records and would liquidate him once they found him. He looked bewildered, because he had to urgently find another home in a safe area. After the collapse of Saddam's regime, many assassination groups had been formed to chase and kill the pilots who had been involved in the war against Iran. People accused some Shia parties of being responsible for creating these assassination gangs, while others accused the Iranian intelligence agency directly for these assassinations. However, there aren't too many differences between the two, and both are probably responsible, since the Shia parties always give their loyalty to Iran as many of them moved there during the period of Saddam's regime, so that Iran became their sponsor. In addition, the ideological similarities between these Shia groups and the Iranian regime consolidated the relationship between them.

Moreover, the pilots aren't the only victims; many people had to change their accommodation to save their lives. The members of Saddam's Al-Ba'ath Party, and those people who had occupied senior positions under his rule, were the first who had moved after the American takeover. The reason for their fear was the revenge of people who had been ill-treated by the previous regime.

The husband of my sister-in-law was one of these people. He had been an officer in the internal police, as well as holding a high position in the Al-Ba'ath party. He had sold his house in New Baghdad City early, to purchase another one somewhere else. But many people had been killed because they had delayed, and hadn't taken the matter seriously.

* * *

In the afternoon I met another cousin of mine. Whilst Sami was closing down his workshop, a small car pulled up opposite the garage gate.

Wahab, who was about forty-five years old, came out from his car and came with opened arms to give me a big hug. His usual smile was marked on his face as always. He still had a stammer in his speech; maybe this deficiency would impart humility to his personality. We had not met since 1984—the year of my father's death when all our kin gathered at the funeral. A woman with a black scarf sat in the front seat of his car. It looked like Wahab had got married, but I didn't intrude or ask because I already knew he was a conservative Muslim, the kind of people whose wives follow a strict Islamic tradition. I would not be surprised if Wahab followed an orthodox Islamic lifestyle because he had been brought up in a very conservative family. His mother, who was the eldest sister of my father, had not revealed her face to any stranger all her life because of the strict rules which had been enforced by her husband. Each one of us talked about what importuned him. Anyway, it wasn't a long conversation, but I noticed that there was a bitter frustration that filtered through his speech.

"They wrapped Iraq in a black huge cloak" said Wahab infuriately. It was easy for me to understand what he meant by a black huge cloak; he was referring to the black clothes which religious Shia's leaders used to wear, as well as black banners hanging on building walls everywhere. It was one of the aspects of Shia's traditions to use those black banners, as well as green flags.

By these colors, they expressed their grief for the death of Imam Al-Husain, the grandson of Prophet Mohammad who had been killed in the seventh century A.D. (680) at Karbala, the holiest Shia's city, 110 Km south of Baghdad. One of the features of grief that Shia showed in mourning the death of Imam Al-Husain was the demonstration of annual rituals that lasted for more than a month. Demonstrators, flanked by audience on each side, walked in a procession, banging their chests violently together with unified, constant rhythm. Some of demonstrators walked in bleeding faces as a result of cutting their shaved heads by blades, while other groups injured their backs and shoulders using chains. From an early age, I used to avoid looking at those rituals, and it was not coincidental that my travel came in this time of the year, when these rituals had already elapsed. I could not blame Wahab for his irritation due to his life circumstances.

All those rituals and ceremonies had been banned in Saddam's days but they burst again into existence with the end of Saddam's regime. Moreover, those bloody celebrations reappeared much stronger than before as a result of the suppression of these rituals for long years. The celebrations began in the first day of Moharum, an Arabic lunar month, when the historical battle Al-Taff between Imam Al-Husain, accompanied by his large family, and the formal army of Al-Kahleefa (the Islamic title for the king or ruler) had taken place in Karbala. The rites, accompanied with traditional slang prose, were being recited in an epic verse to glorify Imam Al-Husain and his family members, who had battled heroically. The lamentation reached its height on the tenth day of Moharum when Imam Al-Husain was killed. After that, people took

to weeping and performing their liturgies for another forty. During the entire fifty days of lamentations, all
aspects of happiness would ban in the Iraqi society. No
wedding ceremonies would be held; no Christmas celebrations, if they fell within Muharram, and no any happy
feasts.

"My nerves are breaking down. I can't bear any more."
Wahab sighed and said in a deep voice. Then he turned to
Sami, trying to drift the speech by asking for some spare
parts to his car.

Most Sunni Muslims looked at these rituals furiously
for being Un-Islamic; as a result, many suicide-attacks
had been occurring every year, targeting the Moharum
rituals. Although there were lots of precautious measures
and plans set up by the government to reduce risks, explosions always took place.

Yet, not all the Shia's demonstrations lacked a source
of pleasure in that some aspects of lamentation were prepared in an interesting theatrical manner to act out the
story of Imam Al-Husain. This rite was the most attractive
thing to me from my early childhood. It was impressed in
my mind the day when a Shia family friend of my parents
invited them to attend this show. Because my father had
a hobby of filmmaking, he was keen to shoot this dramatic activity using his precious 8 mm camera. He took me,
along with my mother, brothers, and sisters, in his station wagon to a barren wide yard crowded with people in
Al-Thawra city, eastern Baghdad, which is now known as
Al-Sadder city. This celebration was called *tashabeeh*, an
Arabic term for "imitations". Many volunteers from the
public came to play a role in the imitation of the battle of
Al-Taff. They used horses and wore historical garments,
carrying swords and shields. People encircled the barren
yard while actors performed what had happened on Karbala more than one thousand and four hundred years
ago. During the performance, a rhapsodist, using a
loudspeaker, recited some prose to explain what was

going on in that battle; meanwhile, the audience shouted in passion and fervor. Actors who performed Imam Al-Husain and his family used to wear black and green colors, while the opponents wore red and yellows colors.

Al-Shimer, the figure who killed Imam Al-Husain, wore all red. As soon as Al-Shimer started to slay Imam Al-Husain, the audience lost control of their feelings and they hysterically began to stone the actor playing his role. As a result, the actor fled away from the anger of the multitude, taking off his red garment while running away. My father tried to find him, hoping to shoot the last scene, but he failed because the person had hid himself from the people.

I always believed that actors who performed the character of Al-Shimer could not be volunteers at all; that it ought to be a good paid job for its risks.

6	# Of Internet and Assassinations	

New Baghdad: July 16th, 2005

Over the next few days, I tried to find an Internet café to do some correspondence. Salim helped me to find one, but it was far away from my sister's house, and his son liked to join me because of his longing to use the Internet. The Internet café was near the Ministry of Culture on a commercial street. I didn't want to go there because of the heavy explosions that rocked that street pretty much every week. However, the Internet café didn't face the main street directly, but was at the back of a building. So I comforted myself that if any explosion occurred, I might be safe.

Getting the Internet in Baghdad was an amazing experience for me because it had been prohibited for a long time during the period of Saddam. During the years I had lived in Iraq, many TV programs, as well as many articles in newspapers, had spoken about the *Internet*, and a lot of effort had been made to explain the advantages of using Internet technology, while nobody was able to figure out what this bloody *Internet* was, because nobody had tried it. I had always thought that not everyone was able to comprehend that mysterious puzzle, but when I left Iraq for Jordan, my opinion changed. I found out that using the Internet was so easy that learning to use it required only a few hours.

The Internet was not the only thing prohibited by Saddam's regime, but mobile phones and satellite TV channels had also been banned.

Playing games online was an amazing experience for my nephew, as it was the first time he had used online games. We spent a couple of hours there, before leaving the café. In the meantime, Salim waited in the street to pick us up in his car.

Anyhow, because the location of this café was unsafe, I kept looking for another one, closer to my sister's home. Eventually I stumbled on a small net café, just a few streets away. A small shop had been adapted to serve as an Internet café, with five computers. I walked every morning to that Internet shop, and browsed the web, despite the jarring noise of the generator that supplied the shop with power. Another generator was set up just a little distance further down, in the middle of the median strip. It was a large industrial one, enough to supply power to a hundred homes, to which it was connected by overhead wires. The intricacy of these wires crisscrossing the street made it too difficult for big vehicles to pass through.

In any case, the Internet shop didn't use this industrial generator, despite the fact that it was very quiet, preferring to use its own noisy one. The front of the shop was a one-way mirror, so that people outside wouldn't be able to see what was going on inside the shop. I couldn't understand at first why the owner used that kind of glass, but day by day, I came to realize that it was some sort of protection against possible aggression. As a result, the owner was able to control who entered his shop. So if he didn't want somebody to get into the shop, or even if he was suspicious, he simply didn't open the door. For this reason, the door was always kept closed and locked, and visitors had to knock and wait until it opened.

These precautionary measures increased my fears, especially when I heard many stories about radical Muslims blackmailing barbers, bakers, and real estate agents, threatening to close their shops. The reason for threatening barbers was that the barbers either "beautify" men or cut their beards, and that is against Islamic Law, according to their interpretation.

Regarding the real estate agents; the rumors were that they were selling properties to Israeli people, but I couldn't understand or find out an explanation for the threats against bakeries. It was easy for everyone to believe these rumors, when many assassinations were occurring every day.

The sound of gunfire could be heard every morning between 7 a.m. and 8 a.m.; this was the sound of the assassinations. No one was able to comprehend why these things occurred at that specific time every morning, but it was certain that shootings were everywhere and people dealt with these events as part of their everyday lives.

One of the victims of these assassinations was my sister's neighbor. I had met that man once, one early morning, when I went with one of my relatives to purchase some buffalo cream. He was a grocer and his shop was close to my sister's house. He was a thin, tall man with a lot of wrinkles on his face. Salim told me that the victim had received a lot of blackmail messages regarding his son, who works in the Iraqi National Guard, demanding his son to resign.

Some assassinations happened just because the people, who had been targeted, were Shia, such as what happened at a bakery, a month before my arrival, when some terrorists attacked it. The attack killed many bakers and most of the TV channels broadcast what had happened. I became sure that no place was secure, no matter where I went, and the only thing I could do was to be more cautious. For this reason, I decreased my visits to that Internet shop, visiting it only for important correspondence.

New Baghdad: July 18th, 2005

During the days I spent in Baghdad, my contact with my wife was made through her sister's daughter.

She failed many times to call via Salim's mobile, or even Sami's mobile, because of inefficient new mobile communication network. She chose to ring her sister's home telephone number to carry her messages for me.

I used to receive a call every two or three days from her nephew, who always invited me to spend some time with her family, as well as delivering my wife's admonitions and fears.

This time I made my mind to call her and appease her fears. Sami advised me to use a specific communication shop in downtown new-Baghdad for its trustworthiness, as he believed.

I took one of the public minivans to downtown and before reaching its destination, I got off it. Here, I had to skirt around the main roundabout before I followed a lane to the communication shop. My memory was still too vivid to recall the great demolition which had occurred on this roundabout, a few months ago, when a petrol truck exploded among a crowd of poor workers. Many TV channels transmitted the horrible images of dismembered, charred corpses from a large number of causalities. I quickened my pace to escape that awful place, looking cautiously at the parked vehicles lest any car bomb crouched besides the curb, though no one could predict where and when those traps would burst.

The communication shop was not roomy. It consisted of a small desk, where a young man sat, a few chairs for customers, and a rare room behind the desk, used as a telephone room.

I gave my telephone number to the man at the desk and he asked me to wait my turn. I took a seat; other waiting customers next to me were chatting loudly. It was a pleasure to listen to their homely, spontaneous dialog and, many times, I barely could conceal my smile. One of the customers was an old villager woman accompanied by a young boy of about twenty. The chat was interrupted when the old villager woman was called to pick up the phone on the desk. She began to talk in a southern rural accent, and her trembling voice showed strong impatience. She was calling her son who had left Iraq to Jordan, where he had found a good job and a secure life after scoring some success as a singer. The young boy with her kept on looking at the customers, pointing at her proudly;

"She is his mother" he said gaily, trying to drag our attention to the woman.

"She is really his mother" he confirmed as he spread a credulous smile on his face, but none of the customers , including me, showed any concern because no one of us had heard of that noteless singer. The village woman spilled much of her enthusiasm when she began to talk about money. Like most of the Iraqi people, she used to receive financial aid every month from her son, and this was the main reason for her call. Mostly, transferring money was done by some small currency exchange shops. For they were lucrative enterprises, they grew fast after Saddam's regime had collapsed, based on the necessity and needs of people to receive money from outside Iraq, after incessant great floods of immigrants were pushed to leave their homes.

It was a new phenomenon that shot up in the Iraqi society in which most families were dismembered to disperse away in two or three counties across the world. Communication shops also spread out quickly in the later years. In New-Baghdad, many new shops were opened as a result of these changes in the Iraqi society. I was able to realize that communication shops along with currency exchange shops were like twins, each one referring to another.

My turn came and I was ushered to use one of the telephones inside the rare room. It was the first time I talked to my wife by phone since I had been in Jordan, before my trip to Iraq. She was worried for me and incessantly forewarned me against the risks of crowded places, and against strolling alone in the streets. I listened and had to submit to her long list of admonitions and instructions, promising her to be cautious. However, my promises did not last very long, and in a few minutes after leaving the communication shop, I accepted that it was in vain following all these precautious rules once I was out, uncovered in the streets. I recalled her admonitions and smiled; thinking of doctors who use to warn their patients to avoid fat and unhealthy foods, but all the instructions shrink once their patients catch sight of tasty foods defying their resistance.

Despite risks in crowded places, they offer gratification for our human nature to be with others as social human beings. The area around the communication shop was well-known to me. Here was an old building opposite to the main road in New-Baghdad. Three upper floors were used as surgeries for private doctors and laboratories. The ground floor had many shops and restaurants. Among these shops, there was a small oriental café. It was my favorite place in the past days where I and my friends from the acting group of New-Baghdad chose to meet after every rehearsal. I halted and looked inside the café. It was a dim view with some barely recognizable, wearisome, untidy men sitting on dilapidated long wooden benches. The clamorous old café, where ebullient disputations on Bertolt Brecht and Jean-Paul Sartre had burst out between the group members, had turned now into a deadened, gloomy place. Now I could only hear murmurs of weary people, probably occupied with how to get their daily food, or how to bear lack of water and electricity. I left the café behind and kept walking on the crowded footpath.

I had to reach the minivan stop on the other edge of downtown. A small bookstall had been erected on the footbath and shrill, zealot Shia songs were coming out from a loudspeaker mounted on its roof. I made a wide curve away from its noise but I was still able to listen to the amateur voices exalting the young religious leader Moktada Al-Sader. Along the footpath, sellers displayed their merchandise, leaving only a narrow pathway to pedestrians, so it was a hard job to split the host and make my way forward. Eventually, I reached the minivan stop. It was a big yard behind an open market. A lot of minivans lined in many queues, and every queue was assigned a specific local suburb, within New-Baghdad city. In vain I tried to find a minivan going to the suburb where my sister lived. Some pedestrians advised me to cross the main road and look around in the other minivan stop. The other stop was assigned for minivans which connected New-Baghdad with other big towns within the great Baghdad. Consequently, I failed to find any local route. Standing immobilized, I looked perplexed to the city in which I had spent most of my life. At length, I stumbled upon that bloody minivan route. It was lined along the main road, away from other minivan stops. When I got in the vehicle, I asked the driver if this was the permanent stop where I could catch the van every day.

"It might be; might not be..." said the driver indifferently.

"They change the stop every week" he added, and turned his face to see how many more passengers were needed to fill his van; some seats were still vacant.

It seemed that my question agitated the anger of the passengers for they began to talk about their weekly suffering with the frequent changes of the minivan stop. Anyhow, I was able to understand that the reason of these changes was there was more than one authority responsible for organizing public transport, and that the religious leader Moktada Al-Sader was in competition with the city government. Therefore, his agency was capable of giving permission to some drivers to use alternative stops.

Moreover, the power of that religious leader extended

into all aspects of life, such as issuing licenses for building or opening shops. Next to the minivan stop, and
behind the open market, many new shops were erected in
an amateur design. About a hundred ground-level shops
were built in four or five lines. Each shop had the same
small narrow dimension as the others. Moktada Al-Sader
gave his orders to build those shops for extension of the
market, though the land where the construction was set
belonged to the new-Baghdad council. It was obvious that
Al-Sader was trying to set himself up as the representative of the popular movement against the emerging
government, and this conflict between the two would-be
governments was one of the many reasons for all this
mess.

Knowing how to reach the public van stops in New
Baghdad meant that I was able to move around by myself
without depending on my brother's car, which was without a license plate. He only used it to drive short
distances, thinking that getting a new plate would cost
him a lot of money. I always objected to using that car,
not only because it was illegal, but also because it was
unsafe.

However, accidents could still happen, even if you took
every possible precaution, and what happened to me on
the next day confirmed this fact. I used a public minibus
to get to my brother Hisham's house. The drivers use a
back street that runs parallel to Channel Street. This
route is used by many of the people who live in the suburbs instead of the main street, so as to avoid driving
close to the American military vehicles. Our driver tried to
overtake a long truck ahead of us, but he couldn't because the truck was carrying long mesh steel, used for
construction, which extended over the back of the truck.
The bus driver attempted to overtake many times, but
there were always other vehicles coming from the opposite direction.

Eventually, the driver made up his mind that he was

going to overtake the truck whatever the consequences, so he increased his speed. Suddenly, an American tank came from the other direction, traveling extremely fast. When the minibus driver tried to retreat safely, he failed due to the length of the truck. The African-American soldier, who stood on top of the tank, aimed his machine gun toward our bus, preparing to shoot, probably thinking it was a suicide bomber. Fortunately, the driver made the right decision quickly, and he turned left heading up the sidewalk. After the tank had passed, the minibus driver sat still for a few seconds before he resumed driving, while the other passengers took a deep breath, and so did I.

7	**Islam & Christianity**	

Baghdad: July 21st, 2005

I went with my mother to visit Hisham, because of his frequent demands that I spend some time with him. The visitors who had come to offer their condolences had all left, and only the family was there. Their daughter-in-law was with them most of the time, as she lived across the street.

When we reached the house, the grieving parents were bursting with anger and frustration. They had just returned from Mosul (Nineveh) where their son's death had occurred. They had lodged a claim for compensation at the American headquarters in Mosul for the wrongful death of their child. After weeks of lengthy procedures, they had been promised compensation of only about 2,500 USD. Fawaz al-Jarba, the parliament member, was luckier than his bodyguards because he was still alive. Besides, he was reimbursed a good amount of money despite the fact that he was a very rich man, and the head of a large tribe.

"I heard that the President of Iraq compensated him with a new 4x4 vehicle in place of the damaged one, as well as the money," my brother said in an angry tone; then added that he thought his son's life was worth more than $2500.

"Poor people are always the losers," I commented.

My brother's wife seized the opportunity to show me a DVD recording of her son's wedding. She looked like she wanted to watch the DVD over again, ruminating on the short, happy memories, as if she had been fond of torturing herself with them. She felt that she and her husband were responsible for the tragic death of her son, because they had agreed for their son to enter such a dangerous career. I was strongly affected by watching a DVD film that showed the happy moments the family had spent cheering and singing; while in the background, the muffled wails of the mother and the young widow could be heard as they watched the film.

* * *

The house was more comfortable than at my sister's, because Hisham used a larger sized generator and was able to power many more electrical appliances. The rooms were all cool because two air conditioners were available. It could also run many lights, a fridge, and two TVs. However, this comfortable house was frequently in need of fuel to run the generators, which added more burden to my brother's shoulders, especially since his income wasn't very steady.

But despite the comfortable house, I didn't like to stay a long time in that atmosphere of grief. The grieving parents used to stay awake every night until 3 or 4 a.m., talking, smoking, and weeping. They remembered their lost son all the time, thinking of the coming grandchild, and hoping that he might be able to make up for what they had lost.

The next evening, Sami joined us, bringing a DVD recording. It was a copy of a debate between the Islamic preacher Ahmed Deedat, and one of the American Christian pastors. Ahmad Deedat was a very famous preacher from South Africa. He had converted to Islam and dedicated all his life to traveling around the world trying to disprove the Bible. I understood that Sami wasn't going to give up and he wanted to stir up religious discussions over and over again, but luck was with me this time, when the cheap copied DVD wouldn't work. It ceased playing many times, giving me the chance to avoid these kinds of discussions, which might have poisoned my relationship with my brother. All the same, my brother attempted to preach to me his Islamic beliefs many times while I was avoiding him. Anyhow, I couldn't stay on neutral ground all the time, so I told him explicitly that the Qur'an had some great verses, but as for some other verses, I couldn't accept them because they encourage violence.

"Look at some of the verses in the Qur'an; they obviously call Muslims to kill everyone who doesn't believe in God or doesn't ban what God and the Prophet Mohammed banned," I said, mentioning verse 29 of Al-Towba chapter in the Qur'an.

"It is not easy to comprehend these verses, you must be wrong in your interpretation," Sami said defensively.

"I have read most of the explanations for this text and I am aware of what I say. The most lenient opinion says that this rule can't apply until the Islamic regime is established. And I can't even accept this idea."

"These are the words of God, and you must show some respect!" he replied in a fury.

"I don't care if they're God's words or the devil's words... I can't accept these kinds of ideas, even if God was incarnated in front of me and ordered me, I wouldn't obey him, and I would tell him, 'Do it yourself. You are God and you can punish your creatures!'" I replied angrily.

"So you don't believe these words but you believe that Christ died on the cross like the Christians believe!" he burst out. "After fifteen centuries from the existence of the Qur'an, you come to contradict it now by saying that Eysa (the name of Jesus according to Qur'an) died on the cross!"

"The Qur'an confirmed that Christ died but you didn't choose the proper interpretation." I referred to some verses in the Qur'an which say in a vague way that God brought somebody else, who was crucified instead of Christ. In fact, these verses are still confusing for Muslims because the Qur'an says in other verses that Christ died and then he ascended to heaven.

"God had replaced Eysa with someone else. The Qur'an says that literally," he stressed.

"How did it happen that all those who were near the cross did not recognize the impostor? His mother Mary, John, and plenty of people too!" I argued. "I assure you, Jesus had died on the cross, and the Bible declared that in many verses, besides several historical references."

"It is not useful to talk with you, your brain has been crammed with nonsense, and may it pay you well!" he sneered at me.

"Do you know what the difference is between you and me? I always use my mind, but you ignore yours," I addressed him sharply, while the argument became very heated. When my mother felt that the argument might lead to something worse, she interrupted and asked us to stop immediately.

That night I felt sorry for the rage I'd showed. I should have controlled myself and not descended into anger. When everybody was sleeping, I seized the opportunity and went to the other room to read from the Bible, of which I had an English copy in my bag. As soon as I opened the Bible, before I chose what to read, Luke 21:16 leapt before my eyes: "You will be handed over by your parents, your brothers and sisters, your relatives, and your friends; and some of you will be put to death." These were the words said by Jesus when he was addressing his disciples. This was a clear message from God, warning me to be wise in my choice of words while in Iraq.

But was it really a message from God? It could have been a mere coincidence. However, from my point of view, it was not. I had been taught by so many experiments how to listen to the voice of God. I would have mocked if someone said that God talks to people, because I had not believed in God at all; but what happened to me after

April 1995 changed my beliefs thoroughly. When my steps led me to one of the Christian churches in Amman, I thought it would be one of those experiments that could benefit me as a playwright.

The smiling people at the gates of the church, who nodded affably, encouraged me to take another step, so that I sat down on one of the long wooden benches, listening to the Christian hymns of the congregation. It was the second time I had ever crossed the threshold of a church; my memory still bore blurred images of a child of eleven years, guided by his mother, ambling with wonder among great pillars in a vast church in Bethlehem. It was the first time I'd ever seen a church in my life, and I had been told later that was in fact the Nativity church.

But the sight now was completely different as the church in Amman was built in a modern style; there were no pillars or huge paintings on the walls; and I was pleased that I should not have to take off my shoes as they did in mosques. It was an Iraqi service that day, and I was invited with my wife to attend this meeting by an Iraqi Christian family. I found out later that the pastor was from Kirkuk city, 280 Km north of Baghdad; and how wonderful it was when I knew that he'd been an actor before becoming a clergyman. Furthermore, many actors who had worked with him on stage were also my friends, as I had lived before in that city. These preliminaries were good enough to break the ice in the first meeting.

While he gave me the Bible to read, I was thinking of the monthly coupons that were given by the church to Iraqi people as international aid. It was my first year in Jordan and the possibility of finding a job was very unlikely with a stagnant economy and soaring unemployment, while thousands and thousands of Iraqis were flowing in every day from Iraq. It was the fourth year of the economic sanctions inflicted by the U.N. against Saddam's regime after the invasion of Kuwait in 1990. People lost any hope of solving the problem and began to forsake their home country, looking for anywhere else in the world, using Jordan as a staging spot.

A widespread rumor in the Iraqi community in Jordan was that some churches facilitated getting visas to Christians to let them emigrate to a safe country. Although the rumor was vague and without much to back it, many Iraqis, and I was one of them, were hoping that it could have been true. This was another reason for me to attend the church every Thursday, as the Iraqi services were being held regularly at that time. Moreover, I was brought up in a family with no fanatical bonds that would have restrained any tendency to adhere to a Christian community. Some images were still haunting me about that little boy who had knelt after his mum to kiss the silver star, beneath the altar in the Grotto of the Nativity Church, which marks the spot believed to be the birthplace of Jesus. Most Muslims glorify these Christian holy places too, as it is part of their beliefs despite the dissimilarities.

When I and my wife returned from the church, we thought it was an exceptional evening and a new experience in our life, but we were still looking at the church as if it was a social club. The Bible that I got from the pastor was laid on the table for a couple of days till my hand picked it up. It was the first time I had held a Bible in my hand, and was different to the one which I had indelibly engraved in my memory.

I remembered a big, old book with a dark cover propped up behind the glass of a dusty display in a small bookshop; I had caught sight of it many times while I was passing by, in one of the main streets in Baghdad long years ago. I always considered it to be a very old book comprised of old superstitions; this was because one of my friends had already read it and told me it was full of vague stories and false notions.

In the small house where I lived in Amman, I was lying on a battered sofa, reading the Gospel. The first impact was marvelous; the verses were loaded with power, as if they were only written yesterday. The teaching of Jesus was such a revolution compared to the conventional stiffened beliefs from my background, and was the way to correct the relationship between God and man, which had been distorted by fanatically religious people.

I still remember the words I said to my wife after I had finished reading it:

"This man says the truth," by which I meant Jesus. In a moment, all the blurred facts about the Bible vanished and the serenity of the soul came to my heart. But, it was only the beginning. At the same time, a converse power tried to snatch the tranquility from my heart by a stream of suspicions and uncertainties like swarms of invisible spirits rushing toward me. I laid the Gospel down and sat up still for a while.

What was that? I thought. I had never, ever read a book like this in my life. Uncertainty about the Trinity and the divinity of Christ were the first things that confused my new-found soul, so I slept that night with this big question upon my mind, waiting for the next Thursday, to hand my questions to the pastor or to one of the elders in the church.

When the time came, and before I asked anyone, the pastor announced the title of his message, which was about the Trinity and the nature of God. *It is mere coincidence, and spares me asking him,* I thought to myself.

The next week, I came to the church with another question and it befell that I heard the answer even before directing my inquiries at anyone. While the pastor was discoursing on a matter which was already in my mind, I was struck by an unknown power trying to draw attention to its existence. It was the same mysterious power I had felt hovering around me in one of Amman's streets a month earlier, when stray winds carried flapping Jordanian Dinar notes above my head to settle under my foot, while I was worried because I had spent the last cent in my pocket. Intrigued by the pursuit of the truth, my concerns of the monthly coupons were disappearing and I grew very interested in discovering this spiritual world. It was not easy to comprehend everything about this creed in just a few weeks, so I kept searching.

I would still receive answers for my questions spontaneously whenever these queries struck me. It took more than three months before submitting to God, and I knelt on my knees, saying:

"Yes...God, I believe you are talking to me, I believe you are a fact and not a superstition."

Since then, the stubborn atheist inside me dropped its resistance to yield the place to Christ, and I learnt that such verses were not mere written words since they carried a great power between the lines.

* * *

My relations with Sami became cold for some time. We didn't get involved in any kind of discussions, nor did he attempt to initiate any. Instead, he gave me a book regarding the duties and responsibilities of Muslims under Islamic law. I realized that he was attempting to offer me a chance to read what he considered one of the Islamic treasures.

I had examined several of these books years ago, especially in Jordan; before getting a job in the radio station, I had had plenty of time to read, benefiting from the public library in central Amman. However, they hadn't attracted my interest, especially those on the subject of religious practices, such as the way of praying or *Al-withou*, which means rinsing some parts of the body with water before prayer. I had always seen these kinds of practices as external forms, thinking that God couldn't be present in these routine rituals.

In any case, the book was so boring that I couldn't finish it. Moreover, some parts were so silly and funny; especially the part telling about an intoxicated man who was brought for judgment to the Prophet Mohammed by some Muslims. When I read that Mohammed ordered his men to beat him with their sandals as a punishment, I burst out laughing while Sami stared at me with annoyance. It was very embarrassing that I couldn't control my laughter, but there was no way to hide what I was thinking, because I believed that it was an eccentric way to deal with an intoxicated man, and that modern life has created a lot of scientific means to treat the addiction.

At any rate, the truce between us didn't subsist for long because my brother wouldn't give up. Two days later, he invited me to join him and visit a café on the Tigris River in Al-Karada district. I guessed it wouldn't only be for entertainment, but rather it would be for a debate. However, I accepted his invitation just for the sake of roaming around Al-Karada district, in which I had spent my childhood.

Another person joined us on our trip out; he was Sami's friend. I had known Habbib for many years as he had always been the best friend to Sami, and their long friendship was based on their mutual beliefs about Islam. Over many years, Habbib had worked alongside Sami, but they had gone their separate ways after Sami's battery project failed a few years ago. As a result, Habbib had bought an old minivan in order to work as a long distance taxi driver between the main Iraqi cities.

It was afternoon and Habbib's vehicle was running through the busy, crowded main street in New-Baghdad. Whenever I was in this street, I always thought that there might be a bomb waiting to explode any time, because many explosions had happened on that street. One of those explosions had taken place a few weeks ago, in which many pedestrians had been killed; even those who were in the upper storey of the adjacent buildings hadn't been safe. One of those victims had been the Ear, Nose, and Throat specialist whom I used to visit many years ago. He was found dead in his surgery on the second floor.

When the minivan left the street safely, I let out a deep sigh of relief as we turned onto the freeway that leads to Karada district. It was a great pleasure for me to see the area where I had grown up and spent my early years, particularly the street where my parents' old house was located. By showing me that street, Sami meant to make me recall my teenage years. I could remember the unforgettable summer days when I used to walk along the street to the Tigris River with my cousins to enjoy a swim.

My father had built the old house on government land and his lease was valid for fifteen years; two of his brothers had done the same. Thus, the street contained three big families living next door to each other. I spent a happy childhood in the company of many cousins, but nothing lasts forever, and we had to vacate our property and move to New Baghdad city when the lease expired.

The car ran on streets that led me deep into my memories. A mixture of pleasure and sadness welled up in my heart, the pleasure of the past and the sadness of the present joining together at a single point.

The landscape of Karada district is magnificent, with the Tigris River curving sharply to embrace the palm trees that cover the area (see p. 183, note #8). At the edge of the district, the freeway crossed a bridge to the other side of the river. Habbib chose to turn under the bridge toward a café located along the river bank.

I was thinking about how I was going to avoid any argument they might initiate. But fortunately, the café workers didn't allow the vehicle to enter the premises since the cafe allowed entrance exclusively for families. But still, Sami and Habbib wouldn't give up, and they were determined to find another café. I didn't know why they insisted on finding a café by the riverbank, but I was curious to know what would happen in the end.

Habbib drove the minivan across the bridge to the other side of the river, but then he turned right and drove parallel to the other river bank, instead of going straight ahead to the southern part of Baghdad. We kept cruising along the river bank past many of the suburbs that hosted the richest and biggest houses in Baghdad. We gradually approached the opposite side of central Baghdad, which is called Bab Al-Moazen. I realized that we had made a half circle around the center of Baghdad. The next suburb on our route was Al-Rahmania, which is one of the most dangerous places in Baghdad. The heavy palm trees in that suburb provide good shelter from which the insurgents can ambush the police force any time. On the other hand, that suburb is also known for the cafés and restaurants that line the riverbank. There were many signs pointing to restaurants specializing in fish barbecue. But although there were so many of them, we couldn't find an open one. Some people had gathered on the pavement just fifty meters from the restaurants, so we parked the car there, hoping to find a café.

The red burning light of the declining sun was coloring the water and the other side of the bank, while a couple of families stood by the river, watching some men and boys who were swimming, braving the dangers around them. We tarried for a while at a wall by the riverbank, which was a short, old fence made of bricks to keep children away from the water's edge. We were still watching the people swimming as we took some rest, and then we moved ahead along the river. The view was breathtaking; it showed the other side of the river where the buildings and mosques of old Baghdad could be seen under the shining crimson sun.

Habbib chose to cross the next bridge to the eastern side of Baghdad, into Al-Adamia District (see p. 180, note #7). He kept driving on the street parallel to the river, but this time, the scene changed because now we were facing the sun directly. The street veered away from the riverside to join with the city, but before reaching the corner, we came to a 4x4 police vehicle parked near a crowd of men sitting on the barrier nearby. Our vehicle could only go forward with difficulty because the police car had almost blocked the road. When we got closer, we noticed that the crowds were drinking beer and enjoying the warm sunset, while a man was selling cans of beer from a wooden cart. I couldn't believe my eyes at first, because drinking beer is forbidden under Islamic law; as a result, all the bars and restaurants that provided drinks had been closed. However, it wasn't impossible to find some men drinking beer in a street, but the amazing thing was to find these people drinking beer under the protection of the police, who were supposed to represent the Islamic government.

I would have liked to have had a beer with those people, but I saw that it wasn't a good idea to expose my thoughts, especially when Sami vilified them, together with the police, because they were committing a sin according to Islamic law.

We left the river behind, as the minivan merged into the city traffic. It wasn't crowded in the city at that time, and most people stayed in their homes because it was unsafe. In the centre of the old city, where the mosque of Abdelkader Al-kaylani attracts thousands of Sunni Muslims, there were only a few pedestrians.

When we reached New Baghdad city, Sami was still looking for a café, but most shops were already closed and darkness was on the horizon. Eventually Habbib drove the car toward the suburb where we lived, and because his house was close to my sister's place, he steered ahead to his house. He parked the van and invited us in for juice. We spent a few minutes inside the house using the pale light coming from the single small lamp, which was fueled by a generator. The air inside was hot, so we moved into the front garden. Eventually, Habbib chose to ask me directly: "What is wrong with Islam that made you unwilling to accept it?"

"Don't you know that your persistent attempts to persuade me about Islam are a kind of intimidation? If we were in Australia, I could sue you," I said, addressing

Sami.

"We're not forcing you. We just want to know what is wrong with Islam," Sami answered.

"I can't have a reasonable discussion because you choose to switch off your mind. You can't discuss anything without a quotation from the Qur'an or the speeches of Prophet Mohammed, Al-hadith, and these quotations are not negotiable, so what are we going to discuss?" I demanded while Sami and Habbib tried to hide their anger.

"But these quotations are the words of God and that is why they are not negotiable," Habbib interjected.

"My mind wants to discuss everything; no holy verses can stop my mind from thinking or negotiating," I said, closing the discussion.

| **8** | # Life with Mortar Bombing | 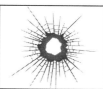 |

Western Baghdad: July 25th, 2005

The persistence of Sami to hold a conversation about Islam and Christianity drove me to look for another shelter away from my sister's home, even for one night. Therefore, I thought that it would be a good time to respond to an invitation from my sister-in-law to spend some time in her home. The suburb where she lived was in western Baghdad, and this had been a good enough reason to defer my visit to her during the previous days, as it was far from New Baghdad. Besides, I could not roam by myself in Baghdad at first.

The minibus carried me to the other bank of Dijla River to pass through the wealthiest suburbs in Baghdad. The streets were very wide and tidy, as were the houses and markets. Because the majority of the people in these suburbs were Sunni Muslims, there were no huge images for holy Muslims—imam—as they were banned by the traditional Sunni community, and this issue is one of the points of contention between Sunni and Shia sects. The green and black flags on top of the buildings disappeared as well, as they also reflected Shia traditions.

My apprehension of facing troubles increased, especially on the main road that led to the Jordanian border (see p. 181, note #5). It could be a hunch, based on the image of the burned American military vehicle I had seen soon after arriving in Baghdad on the same road. The traffic slowed to a crawl, and then stopped, though the road ahead was empty. It was only a few seconds before I saw an American patrol passing along the road. Whenever I came across American force, I feared it might be attacked by insurgents, and if that happened, in most cases, the American force's reaction would have been excessively violent. Because these attacks were unpredictable, soldiers used to shoot with panic in every direction; consequently, many civilians would be killed by mistake. Every week, the media news broadcast a number of such incidents. But everything was all right now, and I took a breath after the detachment had gone away without trouble.

A big mosque on the right side of the road was my landmark to get off the minibus. Suhail, my sister-in-law's husband, was waiting for me in his car on the other side of the road. While we met and hugged each other, I was able to notice some change in his face: it looked pale and flabby as a result of diabetes.

The house was only two hundred meters from the main road. Though Suhail had lost his position as a senior officer in the police force during the period of Saddam, he was still able to purchase this big two-story brick house. His little children had grown up so long ago that I did not even recognize their names.

Ahmed, his elder son, would not get out of the house unless he was sent to buy bread or drove his sister to go to work. His mother, Radyia, who was a teacher in primary school, prohibited him from going out or even from working, saying that it was not secure outside the house at all. In addition to the usual terrors of the outside world, there was another risk threatening this family: the ghost of some Shia gangs pursued Suhail because he had been part of Saddam's internal security system, as well as a member of Al-Ba'ath, Saddam's party. This was enough reason to make them suspect everything.

At night, sitting in the neat front garden with Suhail gave us an opportunity to talk about different topics, but he always interrupted our conversation to listen for something my ears were not able to catch. He would wait for few seconds; his head came up, absolutely motionless, and when he was sure there was nothing to be worried about, he relaxed again to resume talking.

Indeed, I could not blame him, knowing that he had been going through very hard times, especially because some of his relatives were searching for his address. One of their sons had been executed by Saddam's regime, and they believed that he must be punished too, despite that Suhail had not been involved in such a crime. They intended to pass on his new, hidden address to the Shia militia. This was the reason why I had not been given the address on telephone.

Seemingly, his personality had not changed in one or two years, and I was still able to remember his care in locking the main Gate of his old house with a strong chain when he'd still held his position as a police officer. After the invasion of Kuwait in 1990, when everybody thought that Saddam would be destroyed by the coalition forces, all the southern cities had rebelled against Saddam. Suhail had to take off his official military uniform to disguise himself in the dress of a Bedouin, and he fled from the city where he had served.

Although Suhail was from Shia background, he had converted to Sunni many years ago, and this was another reason why his relatives were seized by a deep aversion against him. Converting from Shia to Sunni Muslim did not need special procedures; it required only that the person should keep in touch with the Sunni community by praying in their mosques, as well as using particular names that were exclusively Sunni. Thus, Suhail called his elder son by a Sunni name, and that was enough to allow him to dwell within the Sunni community.

"Do not give my address to anyone... please, whoever asks you, just say that you don't know," he kept repeating over and over.

But whatever precautions were taken by the family to

minimize risks, death could have happened anytime, even indoors. Inside the house, Radyia showed me a small dent in the wall of the living room, where a bullet had penetrated the glass window. It was a result of gunfire in the adjacent street where insurgents and police had fought some weeks ago.

The next morning, Radyia brought a stranger to the house; he was dealing with secondhand furniture and was asked to value the assets of the family. It was the first time when I learnt that they intended to sell the furniture as well as the house so as to leave Iraq. During my previous calls, I'd always encouraged her to take this step, but every time she answered that her family was too big and this was the main obstacle.

In the afternoon, the elder son and his father were ready to go out to pick up the elder daughter from her work. She worked as a sports instructor in the University of Technology, which was close to New-Baghdad. So I thought that time had come to take my leave. Although I'd only spent one night with them, it was a still a very intimate experience.

Before leaving the house, Radyia was very worried and warned her husband to keep clear of the University main gate. After we'd left, I asked Suhail why all these cautions, and he replied that a big explosion had taken place some days ago before the main gate of the university, causing a lot of casualties among the students.

It took an hour for Ahmed to reach the University of Technology, driving the car through the teeming city. At the university, the streets were worse and the car barely moved (see p. 183, note #3). The car drew up by a sidewalk after Ahmed had seen his sister coming from the other side of the road. I *salaamed* (greeted in the Islamic way) and got out of the car to merge into a huddle of people. The shops in front of the university dealt entirely with computer parts. My memory about old times was clear enough to recall some shops offering a copying service to students. I understood that Iraqi people were thirsty for the new technology because they had been deprived of it for a long time.

The shops displayed different kinds of computers. While I was the comparing prices at these shops, an awful muffled sound came and buzzed for a second, followed by a blast. The explosion was feeble, not strong enough to startle me, because the noise of the vehicles in the street was stronger. Spontaneously, people crowded around and spent a while looking at the sky but found nothing until a man announced that a mortar bomb had fallen on one of the houses behind the university. In no more than a few seconds, the people dispersed and went to their jobs as if it had been something quite normal.

Mortars bombs were rather familiar to people in Iraq since some insurgents, benefiting from the easiness of lifting these weapons, shot them at random to land on a target or miss it. I had heard a lot of stories about these 'flying' bombs but this was the first time one fell close to me.

| 9 | **In Search of a Lost Document** | |

Baghdad: July 27th, 2005

The National Theater was my destination this time. The purpose of my visit wasn't to watch a show, but to meet some artists who had been my colleagues before I left Iraq. The National Theater building is one of the significant architectural landmarks in Baghdad. Because the old building for the Institute of Theater and Cinema had been demolished and burned, the workers had to move to the National Theater instead.

The first thing that caught my attention, as soon as I arrived at the place, was the barbed wire surrounding the premises.

I was permitted to pass through the main gate after having been searched by some armed guards. At the main door, other armed guards had already taken their seats and were monitoring the location. Inside the building, the marble floor of the Theater was covered by a layer of dust, as were the walls and furniture. The wide hallway was crowded with employees—people I had never seen before. But I was able to find some of my old colleagues who were excited to receive me. The Theater staff attended work twice a week, but it looked like the administration was just indulging them as they were wasting their time without doing anything except chatting.

For security reasons, the National Theater was unable to present plays in the evenings, so all the plays were performed in the morning, and usually most of the audience were members of the national Theater's staff. It was clear that propaganda was the reason for performing these plays, as if the government was organizing these kinds of activities just to say "The system is working in spite of the explosions!"

However, demanding that theatrical activities continue in the midst of this mess and terrorist attacks was unrealistic. I made this comment directly to the head of the institute, who was my friend. He agreed with me. I was hardly able to find his office, which was on the third storey of the huge, luxurious building. My relationship with him had developed when he'd directed one of my plays in 1985. He looked very tired when I met him, and the years had left his body stooped, which made it difficult for him to walk. He was pessimistic as usual and his opinions about what was happening around us discouraged me from finding any hope for the future. The assistant manager was definitely the opposite extreme, because he was an optimist by nature. He was my friend too, and his optimistic nature gave me hope for the coming times.

"You should share in the rebuilding of Iraq; it's our responsibility," he said, asking me to return to my former position.

I believed his optimistic point of view not because it was based on reality, but because I wanted to. During the years of my exile from Iraq, the dream of coming back to the mother country had never faded. So I acted on his proposal without hesitation, thinking that if it turned out that I couldn't bear the new circumstances, I would be able to leave Iraq at any time. Some of my other colleagues also encouraged me to take this step and return to work, reminding me that if I wanted to stop working, I would have the chance to claim superannuation for the long years I had spent working in Iraqi government departments.

The main obstacle to regaining my previous job was my lack of a records file, since a lot of records had been lost when the Institute of Theater and Cinema was burnt down. Actually, the demolition and burning of the old building was a mysterious incident, because it hadn't been burned as a result of a missile or a bomb attack, but by some unknown people during the early days of the invasion of Baghdad. At any rate, the destruction of this building wasn't an isolated event in those days, as most of the government buildings were burned too. Some of the Theater staff accused the members of Saddam's Bath-party, while some others pointed fingers at the Iranian intelligence, but nobody knew for certain why those buildings had been burned and by whom. It was hopeless to try to retrieve my papers, or to be sure they hadn't been burned, because the Theater office didn't have a computer system for storing files. Moreover, the administrative staff didn't recognize me, as I had left the institute 12 years ago, and most of them were new employees. However, it wasn't the only means available to me to prove my rights. Another option was to go in person and submit a petition to a committee that had been created by the Ministry of Culture. The sole purpose of this committee was to reinstate employees who had been persecuted or dismissed by the previous regime.

Benefiting from my previous work in the radio station in Jordan, I thought that knocking on the door of this committee might be the only way to regain my position, and that the time was due to reap the fruit of my labors. A friend of mine who had worked with me in that radio station advised me to hide my previous activity with that political group, because it hadn't been included in the new governing coalition. I wasn't able to believe that this could obstruct my efforts, thinking that this friend was exaggerating the matter.

Since its old building had been abandoned, the Ministry of Culture had moved into the offices of the Iraqi Fashion Design Institute. It was a huge building with several stories and many wings; all of it had been made in a distinguished architectural style. This building was one of many which had been constructed under the supervision of Saddam Hussein, as he was interested in architecture.

Fortunately, I was able to find an old friend who led me to the committee's office on the third story. The office had a small desk with an average-looking woman sitting behind it; she was the committee coordinator. She gave me a poorly photocopied one-page form, telling me to fill it in and hand it over at the committee meeting, which was held once a week.

My old friend invited me to visit his office, which was on the ground floor. He now held the position of an editor for a weekly cultural magazine belonging to the Ministry.

At his office, there were many things to talk about, because we had lost contact with each other for many years. He looked dissatisfied regarding my desire to stay in Iraq, but he didn't like to interfere with my decision. In any case, I wasn't a hundred percent sure myself that I had made the right decision. I just wanted to let things take their course, and see what might happen.

Baghdad: July 30th, 2005

Over the following days, I tried to get a hold of any documents that might prove my rights as a previous employee of the Institute of Theater and Cinema, but I found none. The main document I had to rely on was the form that I had received from the committee coordinator. Now I needed to find two employees to bear witness that I had previously been employed by the Institute. It didn't take much effort to find the two witnesses, since the Theater manager and his assistant were both ready to sign the form declaring that I had been on the Theater payroll before 1994.

This was the good news; the bad news was that a great explosion occurred in front of the building of the National Theater, killing seven and wounding twenty-six people[6].

---

6 "Bombs kill 2 British guards, 7 Iraqis; constitution date looms". *The*

That morning I went to the Theater to finish the reinstatement process, but as soon as I arrived, I saw broken glass strewn all over the Theater courtyard; it had come from the wide front windows of the building, which had all been broken.

As soon as I entered the hall, some workers told me that a suicidal radical Muslim had set off a car bomb in front of the premises the day before. The vehicle must have been carrying a large amount of explosives, since it caused huge damage to the surrounding buildings. Fortunately, the explosion had occurred on a holiday when nobody was in the Theater, and for this reason, the casualties were from nearby pedestrians. Inside the building, some employees were still cleaning the broken glass from the ground. The large broken windows, which faced the main street, were curtained with plastic covers to protect the inside from the hot dusty winds blowing usually in summer. The manager was calling the Deputy Minister while I entered his office; he was giving him an estimate of the amount of money needed to fix the broken windows. I thought that he was going to oppose my desire to stay in Iraq, or that he would at least have a comment to make about it. But he didn't. He wrote me a good reference and then went back to work as usual. Meanwhile, one of the employees was telling him about the terrorist's severed head, which had been found on the upper roof of the Theater building.

That evening, I was at my sister's house watching the TV news and it showed the great explosion in front of the National Theater. I didn't tell anyone in my family about the things I was doing to get back to work, because I wasn't sure whether my claim would be approved. Besides, that explosion was like a warning bell, telling me to review my decision, but I wanted to know the results of my claim.

Post-Standard. 07/31/2005. AP Wire report by Bassem Mroue.

Baghdad: August 3rd, 2005

On the day when the committee meeting was to be held, I waited my turn in front of one of the ministry's rooms on the ground floor. Many people were gathering to wait their turn, as the procedures were very slow. I was able to peek inside to see what was happening whenever the door swung. The committee consisted of only one man, whose face was rather familiar to me. I couldn't quite remember who he was, but I was able to recall that he used to be one of the employees of the Theater and Cinema Institute years ago. In any case, I was certain that he hadn't held an important position. My friend, the editor, met me while I was waiting my turn. We had a quick conversation before he went to his office, but I sensed from his expression that he wanted me to call off my plans to stay in Iraq. Eventually, my turn came to enter the room and to stand right in front of the man who was the whole committee. He avoided looking me in my eyes and continued scrutinizing my papers, which had been put on a small table in front of him.

"Had anybody in your family been executed or put in jail under the previous regime?" he asked formally, pretending he didn't recognize me.

"No, but I personally was chased by Saddam's agents in Jordan because I was working for a radio station belonging to the Al-Wifaq opposition group," I answered.

"You can't call this kind of work resistance activity; it was just a way to earn enough money to keep you alive" he said dismissively.

"No it wasn't just to earn money. My life was indeed in danger, and my family suffered because of my work for this radio station. My brother was interrogated many times by the local agent of the Al-Ba'ath Party and the interrogator showed him my name, which had been listed with people who were sentenced to execution." This was just what my brother Hisham had revealed to me.

"Do you have a copy of that list?" he replied.

"No," I answered him, thinking I should walk out of the room, but I decided that I should exhibit more patience.

"You know that this committee was established for people who were persecuted by the previous regime, and without any proof of persecution, it will be difficult to do anything. There is another thing—you can't prove that you were employed by the Theater and Cinema Institute."

"Aren't these documents enough?" I said, and laid down in front of him the programs for my many plays that had been performed by the national Theater group.

"I know you, Sir, I know you were a playwright, but that doesn't prove that you were an employee."

"The manager and assistant manager have given evidence and confirmed that I was an employee in this institute," I replied, preparing to leave the room.

"I am sorry, this evidence is still not enough," he said.

I left the room, thinking that I had wasted many years of my life working with one of the opposition parties, and blaming myself for ignoring the advice of my friend who had told me not to reveal my relationship with the Al-Wifaq group. It was not a secret to know that the man who had interviewed me had unlimited authority, maybe more than what the Minister had, and I made sure of this fact later when I knew that he was from the Shia parties in the coalition and the Minister wasn't.

Many lists were pinned up on a board in the Ministry's wide main hall. They included hundreds of names of people who had been reinstated by the committee. The reason for reinstating them was that they had been persecuted by the previous regime, as was written on the top of each list. I scrutinized the list for the Theater and Cinema Institute carefully. I was able to recognize many of those names, but I was sure none of them had ever been involved in any political activities. One of the names was my brother-in-law's wife; she had worked as a technician and had left her job because of her obligations to her kids. However, she had already told me that she had got a recommendation from the main Shia party, proving she had enrolled in that party, despite being a Sunni.

Before I left the Ministry building, I met my friend, the editor, at the end of the corridor. He expressed his sympathy and advised me to spit on Iraq and leave.

10 | North to Kirkuk

Baghdad: August 6th, 2005

I had put Kirkuk in my original itinerary and I never stopped thinking about visiting there. I had left many of my best friends behind in that city, besides a lot of beautiful memories, which I still carry with me wherever I go. In that city, I had taken my first steps in my field of work, putting into practice what I had learnt at the university.

I delayed visiting Kirkuk because I was very cautious about travelling outside Baghdad until I had fully prepared myself for the dangers that lurked everywhere. But gradually, I learnt to overcome my fears so that I found myself paying less and less attention to the risks around me. My mother refused to let me travel by myself so she insisted on joining me, thinking that I would be safe if I was accompanied by her. In the early morning, Salim gave us a lift to Al-Nahda, the central bus station. This is the departure point from which most public transport vehicles set off on their journeys to all the cities of eastern Iraq. Thousands of people from various places gather there every day to travel to the north-eastern and the south-eastern cities.

My memories of this station were quite fresh and the images of past days welled up in my mind, reminding me of the time of the Iran-Iraq war. In those days, this place used to be crowded with soldiers, struggling for any transport to convey them to their military camps because transportation in wartime was very scarce. But now, everything had changed and no one wore military clothes because all the passengers were civilians. Moreover, there were plenty of buses and vans waiting for someone to fill their empty seats. We chose to take a big bus, though it was slower than a van. My mother preferred this kind of transportation because it had an aisle between the seats so passengers could stretch their legs during the journey.

While the bus was passing through the outer suburbs of Baghdad, I noticed that they had been extended and had become more crowded than before. Many things had changed, but it was hard to know precisely what they were, because the bus was travelling fast. However, what especially attracted my attention was a new mosque that had been built in a marvelous architectural style. It might have been built in the last years of Saddam's rule, so that I hadn't seen it before. The mosque was located at the intersection of four main roads; one of them led to the north-eastern cities.

Because the morning sun shone into my eyes, I adjusted the dirty curtain of the right window beside me. I tried to enjoy a light nap but I wasn't able to sleep. So, from time to time, I pulled back the curtain, just to have a look outside. Nothing important had changed on that road, which I had travelled hundreds of times before. The first time was in 1978, when a letter from the ministry of education summoned me to work in Kirkuk as an arts teacher in a secondary school. I was one of many graduates who had been selected to work in Kirkuk, not because of our excellence, but because of our race. At first, I didn't realize the reason behind this, but over time, I found out it was one of the first steps in a plan by the Iraqi leadership to increase the Arab population in Kirkuk city, because its population mostly comprised Turkmen and Kurds.

Because it was the first job offer I had ever received, I accepted it without hesitation. Another reason encouraging me to consent was that my compulsory military service would be deferred for three years if I accepted to work as a teacher. Due to the lack of secondary school teachers, new legislation had been introduced to encourage new graduates to fill teaching vacancies. Thus, if I had rejected the job, I might have been drafted into the army.

Anyhow, I thought it would be only for one year, and then I could hand over a claim to the ministry of education to move to Baghdad or any nearby city. But two years passed and nothing happened. Eventually, I realized that I was one of many who were part of the government's plan to change the entire demographic of Kirkuk city.

In 1980, the Iraqi leadership's plan became more obvious, when the government began to take action on the ground in Kirkuk. One day, the governor of Kirkuk, with the leader of the local Al-ba'ath Party branch, called all the Arabic teachers and government employees who had been born outside Kirkuk, to a large meeting. Even before the day of the meeting, rumors had been spreading about the government's policy of facilitating the settlement of Arabs in Kirkuk. However, everything was revealed at the meeting, when the governor announced the plans to create incentives for Arabs to put their roots in Kirkuk.

The government's plan included granting every new settler a piece of land, as well as a sum of money—ten thousand Iraqi dinars—to help people build their new houses. The offer was conditional on the person transferring his records from the population register of his home city to Kirkuk. In fact, it wasn't easy for someone who was just starting out in life to resist this offer. Moreover, the leader of the local Ba'ath Party emphasized during the meeting that we had no chance of moving back to our original cities whether we accepted the offer or not, because a decision had already been taken by Saddam Hussein to obstruct the movement of any government employees out of Kirkuk.

I had thought that I would be able to take advantage of

the money by seizing the opportunity to study in an American university, the dream that I had always had. But the winds blew against my ships, as Arabs say, when the war broke out between Iraq and Iran, and the Iraqi border was sealed, robbing me of the opportunity to chase my dreams because that war continued for eight years.

However, the ten thousand Iraqi dinars I had received wasn't a treasure in Saddam's days because exchanging currency was prohibited without special permission, so that the only thing I was able to buy was a used car. I wasn't even able to start any construction on the land that I had received without getting a loan from the bank. I couldn't complete the building either, in spite of getting the loan, so that my unfinished home remained abandoned.

In fact, looking for my half built house had been the main reason for my visiting Kirkuk, even though there was little hope of finding the property. This is many abandoned buildings had been requisitioned by Saddam's regime and granted to other people.

The bus stopped in Tuz Khurmatu city, eighty kilometers from Kirkuk (see p. 187, note #1). During the four hours of driving between Baghdad and Kirkuk, most drivers got their rest at this small city, using many restaurants along both sides of the main road. The majority of people in this city were Kurds, besides Arabs and Turkmen. Because of the surrounding mountains, the city had always needed a permanent military presence to keep them under Saddam's control, but beyond those mountains were many Kurdish villages, which had always been considered as Kurdish insurgent territory. It was clear that the city had now given its loyalty to the Kurdish leadership thoroughly, because no sign was written in either Arabic or Turkmen, but only in Kurdish, which was the only language used. Also, I saw huge images of the Kurdish leaders along the main road.

This main road was the most dangerous place in the city, and many explosive-filled vehicles had detonated over the past few months against these restaurants where the drivers would park. For this reason, I disliked staying in this place, and wanted to leave at once. Anyway, I wasn't able to leave by myself because I had to stay with the other passengers who got off the bus to have their meal. Even though I wasn't hungry, I preferred to have some food, thinking that my mother might want to have her lunch. The food wasn't tasty and it had been hastily prepared, not to mention the high cost despite the poor quality. The only one who enjoyed the food was the driver, because he didn't pay a cent. As an experienced traveler on this road, I knew that every driver had an unofficial verbal agreement with one of the restaurant owners. Due to this agreement, every bus driver got a free special meal when he brought along his busload of customers.

Kirkuk: August 6th, 2005

It was 2 p.m. when the bus approached Kirkuk city. I planned to stay with one of my dearest friends, Aziz, instead of a hotel. I had already attempted to contact him but I hadn't been able to find a way to do that, as I had lost his telephone number many years ago. However, I decided that as soon as I arrived in Kirkuk, I would go straightaway to his house to visit, even though I wasn't sure if he still lived there, or even if he was alive at all.

During my long residence in Jordan, I had thought many times about contacting this friend, as well as my other friends and relatives. But because of my previous work with the opposition group, I thought that they might be interrogated by the authorities, because most of the international calls were being spied on by Saddam's intelligence.

It looked like the main road leading to the center of Kirkuk had changed, since a new bridge was being built here, and also many intersections and buildings had gone up. The driver drove the bus through a new street I hadn't seen before while I was digging through my memories, trying to get a sense of where we were. Finally, the bus stopped at the terminal, which wasn't familiar to me. I spent a couple of minutes trying to make out the area, but eventually worked out that I was standing beside the old central bus station which had been renovated and completely transformed.

The temperature was over forty degrees of Celsius (104 degrees Fahrenheit), as if it was June. But in spite of this hot weather, looking at the quiet, clean city and comparing it with Baghdad gave me some comfort. We rented a taxi and headed toward the suburb in which Aziz lived. As my mind began to resolve the indistinct pictures around me into the images of the old city features and streets I once knew, a sense of relief crept up inside me.

The old suburb where Aziz lived was still very poor and no signs of renovation could be found on either side of the old street. The buildings, the old mosque, the stripped football playing field, nothing had changed, not even the cracked street which we were using. As a result, it was easy to define the locations without any effort, and I was able to find Aziz's house easily since it was on the main street of the suburb. When I knocked on the main iron gate, his daughter hurried to open it; she was now eighteen years old.

"Can't you remember me? Call your mother," I said, while her mother was coming over from the kitchen, which was near the main gate. As soon as Aziz's wife looked at me; she recognized me, received me with a warm welcome, and invited me, together with my mother, into her home.

The hall was still as simple as it had been before, except for a new wall unit, which contained a new television. There were no chairs or sofa in the room, but some single thin mattresses had been laid out along the edges of the room for sitting, like in most Iraqi villagers' sitting rooms. A large portrait of Aziz, which was hanging on the wall, showed a lot of changes in his features. He was at work, so his wife did her best to offer the proper hospitality. She still kept her Iraqi village manners, which dictate that guests must be welcomed warmly and provided with food, drink, and a comfortable bed.

I had lived with this family for many months before leaving Iraq and they had treated me as though I were one of the family. Actually, this was what had encouraged me to choose to reside with them instead of staying in a hotel. Besides, it was the safest to stay in a private home. Moreover, my mother was very comfortable and she was able to feel at ease very soon.

When Aziz returned home, he looked very similar to his portrait; the gray color on his hair and the wrinkles on his face giving him a stern appearance. During the eight years that I'd lived in Kirkuk, I had known him as one of the most brilliant theatrical actors in the city. His satirical sense of humor was the most salient character trait, significant despite his sullen, stern face. I was surprised when he told me that he was lecturing in drama at a fine arts school, since it was the first time I had heard about a new school for fine arts in Kirkuk. But this job wasn't the only means by which he earned his living, because he had to work at many part time jobs to be able to provide a decent standard of living for his large family. He worked in a radio station in the morning, as a lecturer in drama in afternoon, and as a Theater director in the evening. He had to do all these jobs in order to be able to discharge his family's obligations, especially after the death of his younger brother, who had passed away a year ago, leaving behind many children who had to be nurtured. I was really saddened by his death as he had died at the young of forty. The story I was told was that he had been complaining of symptoms of high blood pressure, but it was his carelessness in taking his medications that led to his death.

My mother thought that we shouldn't waste time, so

she insisted on searching for my unfinished house, even though it was only my first day in Kirkuk. Aziz was pessimistic about the possibility of finding the house, telling us that most of the abandoned houses had been taken over by the previous regime and given to other people. He thought that even if it was still legally mine, it wouldn't have remained intact because many abandoned houses had been stolen piece by piece many years ago. It was easy to believe his point of view because theft of construction materials was common in Saddam's days, when their prices had soared as a result of the economic sanctions against Iraq.

However, all these arguments weren't sufficient reason to stop searching for the house, but I realized that Aziz wasn't the right person to support me in my endeavors, as he was an indolent man by nature. Therefore, I thought about asking another friend, Ali, to help me.

Ali was an actor too and lived in a nearby suburb. His hair had gone white in his youth, and he was well known for his distinctive appearance. At sunset, the heat became bearable, so we thought it was a good time to go out looking for Ali because he had moved. Ali had never expected to find me standing in front of his house and he greeted me very warmly. He used to live in a building next door to his current dwelling, but I was astonished to see that the place where he lived now had once become a big store belonging to Kirkuk Council. Ali had renovated his current house to accommodate his family. When the governmental complex in which he used to live had been sold at auction, he found that he wasn't able to purchase the unit, so he had made an appeal to the council to let him use this abandoned store opposite it as a temporary solution for his family. Afterward, when the previous regime had collapsed, he decided that it was a good opportunity to build some internal walls, dividing the huge store into two bedrooms, a hall, a kitchen, and a bathroom.

Anyway, his story was a result of the extraordinary circumstances in which Iraqis were now living, and it was not unique. After the collapse of Saddam's regime, thousands and thousands of poor families had occupied government buildings to dwell in, and some of them obtained permission from some effective religious leaders, so no one could get them out.

As I expected, Ali was a diligent, industrious person, and he hurried to help me as soon as I asked him. Using his old car, he drove me, with my mother and Aziz, and searched the area, which had thoroughly changed because all the empty spaces had been built upon. The small street leading to the old timber mill was my landmark, since my house was close to it. My house was halfway down a short street about two hundred meters away. I couldn't believe my eyes when I found it intact, but I noticed that the ground had been leveled with earth and put right. Besides, some signs showed that it was occupied.

Houses in Iraq are usually identified by a number plate. Although this house lacked one, I was able to check it was my house by following the consecutive numbers of the surrounding houses.

It had happened that the neighbor, who was an Arabic man, had used my unfinished house to provide accommodation for his married eldest son for many years, and that was the reason why the house hadn't been looted.

When we met the father, he treated us rudely and he insisted that I wasn't the real owner, and even though I showed the evidence of my ownership, he still persisted in arguing that it wasn't really mine. However, he mentioned off-handedly that he might try and request official verification from the Department of Properties Registration. It was obvious that the man was lying and trying to keep the use of the house for himself as long as possible. Anyhow, I realized that a lot of difficulties might await me in solving this problem.

Surrounding my house were many abandoned unfinished buildings that had been claimed by some Kurds, who had put up warning signs to keep away intruders, with Kurdish letters in red paint. Ali translated these words for me, as he knew Kurdish. They were a sort of blackmail, addressing the Arab owners to force them to leave their properties. Generally, Kurds believe that those Arabs had been used by the previous regime to change the demographics of the city. As a result, the Kurds were attempting to take up every house that became available among the Arab dwellers with the aim of 'recouping' these properties, even though Kurds hadn't owned them previously. This atmosphere was bringing dark clouds over the place, and over me.

Ali suggested asking his brother-in-law, Abdullah, who was a property lawyer, so that I could be certain if I was the sole owner or if I shared the ownership with someone else. In fact, a lot of property quarrels had happened after the collapse of Saddam's regime, so that the new authorities had been obligated to set up a new court restricted only to solving these quarrels. I was sure it would be a very complicated process if I lodged a claim with this court, because there was a great backlog of cases to be heard.

11	### The Shadow of the Past	

Kirkuk: August 8th, 2005

Ali invited me with my mother to have lunch at his home. In the meantime, he gave Abdullah the serial number of my property to verify from the records. We were sitting on the floor in a circle around the food, like most Arabs do when they eat, when a handsome young man came into the house with a smile on his face. He was Abdullah, whom we had been waiting for, and he assured me that the property was still in my name according to the government records.

Things turned out to be much clearer after I verified that I was the sole owner of the property, and so my main mission in Kirkuk now was to sell the property as fast as I could.

Now that she could be certain that I would be safe with my friends, my mother preferred to travel back to Baghdad. Next morning, Ali drove her in his car to the bus station and Aziz accompanied us to see her off. The streets weren't overcrowded like they were in Baghdad, and the American military vehicles were less aggressive in their dealings with other people and traffic. I was surprised when I saw that the cars were able to approach the military vehicles with no fear. Being absent-minded, Ali nearly made a serious mistake on one of the intersections when he got too close to an American military vehicle. Fortunately, he stopped his car just in time before crashing into the military vehicle, which was just two meters away from our car. I thought if this thing had happened in Baghdad, we would all have been killed.

We left the bus station behind and headed downtown to the popular old café near the main bridge in the middle of Kirkuk, where most members of the theatrical community would meet every morning. It was a regular morning ritual for all the actors who still resided in Kirkuk, where they would discuss their plans for the coming day. Nothing had changed about that old café; the wooden benches, the people and my favorite black tea were all still the same.

A pleasant sense of nostalgia crept over me when I recognized something of the old Kirkuk still living among these aged wooden benches. Also, I thanked God that my two best friends in Kirkuk had kept their enthusiasm for the Theater, instead of turning to religious fanaticism like most of the people I had met.

It was 10 a.m. when Aziz left the café for work. His working day was a long one, divided between a local Kurdish TV station and the school of fine arts. After a while, Ali left the café too, so I had a chance to walk around downtown Kirkuk by myself.

On the ground level of a commercial building, on the opposite side of the old café, was a government office set up to provide the public with communications facilities. The new Internet service which had been set up in this location enticed me across the threshold. It was air conditioned, so I stayed inside and used the Internet because the weather outside was very hot. About ten computers had been arranged along a large hall; they were of good quality as was the Internet connection. I was able to successfully contact my travel agent to delay my return flight as I planned to stay another month before setting off on my long travel back to Sydney.

Along the bank of the Kakasasu, the Turkish name given to the canal that divides Kirkuk in two, some summery bars had been erected, adding a distinctive aspect to the city. I was surprised to see these bars selling alcohol without any ban or obstructions. As I walked ahead, the main commercial street was crowded with people, and the shops were selling every kind of goods. Indeed, the manner of life in Kirkuk was surprisingly different from that of Baghdad. The most striking example of this was the electric power supply, which was provided to houses by the government for more than twelve hours each day. Even petrol, which was causing a daily crisis in Baghdad, was available in Kirkuk because the government was providing all drivers with a monthly coupon to ration fuel consumption. I guessed that the Kurdish leadership was trying to persuade the local Arab community in Kirkuk of the advantage of making Kirkuk part of the Kurdish regions.

On the other hand, life in Kirkuk was still full of ever-present dangers and many explosions had occurred there in the last month. One of those explosions had taken place in front of the main Rafidain Bank near the old café. The signs of that explosion were still now visible on the bank walls and the ground as a reminder of the awful crime, which had killed twenty-two and wounded eighty people while pensioners were standing in line to receive their monthly payments from the bank.[7]

All explosions, excluding that one, had been directed at the American army as well as the local police force, which consisted entirely of Kurds. Since the Arabs were the big losers from the changes in Kirkuk, fingers were always being pointed at them in accusation over such attacks. Moreover, the religious factor provided a further reason to blame the Arabs in Kirkuk, because most of them were Sunni Muslims, and had thus been already branded as rebels.

In the afternoon, I spent a lot of time at Ali's house. Near his dwelling, a small space of land had been turned into a garden containing many kinds of vegetables. The

---

[7] "Suicide Bomber Kills 22 in Attack at an Iraq Bank", *New York Times*, 06/15/2005. Terry Wong.

garden was fenced with barbed wire to keep the neighbors' children from entering it. Ali looked very proud as he showed off his garden with its many plants, thinking he had accomplished a lot in transforming this small space from a dump, where the neighbors used to get rid of their rubbish, into a beautiful garden.

Ali's house and the surrounding buildings stirred up memories of the unforgettable events of the first Gulf War in 1990. Everything around me called up images of the stolen properties which had been taken from Kurds who had fled away, leaving Kirkuk to Saddam. When Saddam's army had been forced out of Kuwait, the Kurds had seized the opportunity to take over Kirkuk because they thought that the Iraqi force had been completely destroyed. But when the army had regrouped and regained its strength, all the Kurds fled to the northern Kurdish cities, leaving their houses to be looted.

In those days, I had finished my compulsory military service in a local military newspaper in Baghdad and I had been required to return to my former position as a secondary school teacher in Kirkuk. There was no petrol available for private usage because all fuel had been reserved for the military, so it wasn't easy to find a means of traveling to Kirkuk. But eventually I had stumbled on a military journalistic group going to Kirkuk in a land cruiser to cover the events, and since I had served with them at the same newspaper, they felt obliged to take me with them.

The car had to use the northwestern route, passing through Tikrit, the city of Saddam's birth, as the main road to Kirkuk was blocked by the Kurdish forces (see p. 186, note #3). It was safer because it mainly passed through cities loyal to Saddam at a time when most of the northern and southern cities were in open rebellion. Before reaching Bajey City, eighty kilometers north of Tikrit, the car stopped to fill up at a petrol station which belonged to the army. When we reached Bajey, the driver turned right into another road, which led to Western Kirkuk. This route was much longer, because it was impossible to travel by the normal road to Kirkuk since its southern part, which passes through mountains, was still dominated by the Kurdish forces.

It was a while before we reached Al-Hawija, thirty kilometers west of Kirkuk. As we traveled these thirty kilometers, I observed the huge military forces, deployed on both sides of the road, comprising the modern Russian-built T-72 tanks as well as a large number of Multiple Barrel Rockets.It was clear that the collapse of Saddam's army, which we had all watched on television, hadn't really happened. He was still strong enough to regain Kirkuk and the other rebellious cities.

When we reached the main intersection in Kirkuk, I got out of the vehicle, leaving the journalists behind. I had to walk because there was no hope of finding any transportation, in spite of the fact that it was early afternoon.

The air was rich with the stench of blood and some traces of blood spots still remained on the street despite the efforts having been made to wash them. I crossed the main bridge to the other side of the city, passing through the old vegetable market. Not many people were there, but gradually the city was beginning to resurrect itself and I could see some men appearing out of their houses.

The first friend I had ever met in Kirkuk was a teacher, who had been working with me at the same school. At the time, he lived in the building which I could now see, standing on the opposite side of the street with Ali. That day back then, when I'd met this teacher, he was pushing a wooden wardrobe into his apartment. He told me that the Kurds had stolen his furniture while he was away from Kirkuk and he was taking back his property. Other people were searching through other apartments that had been deserted by Kurds who had fled for fear of the revenge of Saddam's army.

There was no need to drive the Kurds out of Kirkuk

when Saddam's army took the city back, because they had already fled their suburbs. This gave people the opportunity to rush into these suburbs looting and stealing. I was one of the witnesses who had seen these terrible days first hand. When Adil, one of my old friends, had called me to join him to go to Al-Shorja, the main Kurdish suburb in Kirkuk, I went with him out of curiosity to know what was happening there.

When we reached Al-Shorja, the army was besieging the area, combing all the streets. So, no one could get in or even approach it very close. There were crowds of people watching curiously on the edge of the suburb. Having searched the area, the soldiers hastened to loot the small valuable items before they got in their military trucks, giving way to the rabble, who hysterically rushed into the suburban houses. Because of the lack of fuel to operate vehicles, people used carts pulled by donkeys and horses to carry the stolen property, while others had to push or drag their loot along the road. Some of them had realized along the way that the stolen items were too heavy and they wouldn't be able to carry on, so they got rid of what they were carrying to return for another raid. Along the main road, which led to that suburb, a lot of fridges and heavy furniture had been dropped by the roadside and people were hurrying frantically in all directions.

I was standing with Adil watching all this chaos, when he walked toward the deserted houses, calling me to follow him. I thought we shouldn't step any closer so I stayed immobile, but he kept calling over and over again, asking me to have a look at what was going on inside those houses. The open doors and the rushing people lessened my embarrassment, so I followed him in bashful steps, looking around me every second lest some acquaintance would see me. Adil was quite unlike me, as he had enough courage to rush into those houses without hesitation. Inside there, people were scattering the furniture, searching for anything valuable. It was clear that a lot of those who had left their properties were loyal to Saddam, even though they were Kurds, because they had hung big framed photographs of Saddam on the walls.

When Adil began to join in with the other people, I warned him not to take anything, but even while I was warning him, I found myself instinctively drawn to take some tools that were strewn on the ground. I thought I could use them for my car. Such a strong sensation filled me as though there were sort of invisible evil spirits hovering around the place; and some mysterious power was gradually driving me to look for more lightweight items and start moving from house to house with searching eyes, to join the rabble and abandon any moral considerations. However, after I was able to regain control of myself, I realized I should get rid of anything in my hands and leave that place immediately.

All these images had been conjured up in my mind while I stood beside Ali, who was watering his neat garden.

"Hey... come over here; have a look," he called me delightedly to show a big watermelon tucked away under leaves.

* * *

In the early evening of the same day, Ali took me in his car to search for a real estate agent to advertise my property. It was a very hot day and this was the right time to go out; all real estate agents and shops would open after they had spent a long break during the lunch interval. I already presumed that selling would not be an easy assignment, and there would be trouble ahead, despite the positive results of our efforts to verify my ownership of the property. However, I wasn't inclined to get involved in any kind of quarrel, especially when the law was out of reach.

We didn't have any specific agent in mind, but we thought that a Kurdish broker might be preferable because only Kurds were interested in purchasing property in Kirkuk.

In fact, from the first days of liberating Iraq, the Kurds had been trying to conquer Kirkuk by any means possible. For this reason, the Kurdish leadership had encouraged Kurds, wherever they were, to settle in Kirkuk by providing a lot of incentives for them, such as making it easier to obtain a piece of land for free, as well as granting them some money toward the construction of their houses.

It was understandable that the Kurdish leadership followed the same strategy that had been practiced before by Saddam. They were also conducting a propaganda campaign in their media to convince Kurds of their rights in Kirkuk; and thus, to secede from the Arab territories and join the city to the Kurdish regions.

We found a real estate agent, although he was located a long way from my property. Ali helped me by interpreting since he spoke Kurdish too, like all native Arabs in Kirkuk. We explained all the details of the property, including its location and measurements, but as all brokers had done, the agent quoted a low price. I didn't want to get involved in any negotiation with the broker because I wasn't certain yet of the local prices, but I realized that if I wanted to get a higher price, I should stay longer in Kirkuk. The agent promised to look for a buyer in about a week and finally, he mentioned that I might be able to get a better price.

Kirkuk: August 9th, 2005

In the afternoon, Aziz and Ali invited me to join them for a meeting to be held in the office of a local newspaper; it would discuss some local theatrical issues in Kirkuk.

After they led me through a narrow lane, not far from the city centre, we stopped at a small old building consisting of a few apartments. I guessed that the place was located in one of these units. They said that they would wait for Raad Mutasha Al-Issawi, the Editor-in-Chief, to open the door.

Because he used to work in the theater in Kirkuk, Raad was offered the newspaper's office for the theatrical affairs committee meetings. I had heard a lot about his activities before I met him as he used to publish many articles and poems in different papers; but also for his other contributions in the Iraqi Theater as a playwright. Besides his job in his small local newspaper, he was the manager of information in the Governor's office and the head of the union of writers in Kirkuk.

This long list of jobs needed a man who had exceptional abilities, and that was what I guessed before I met him. A few minutes later, a four-wheel drive SUV stopped close to us and Raad got out it. He was about forty years old, a handsome man with dark brown skin and black hair. The thing that struck me was a big automatic pistol holstered in his belt, which confused the picture of the writer and poet that I'd already drawn in my imagination. He introduced himself to me, welcomed me very warmly and asked Ali to interview me for his paper. In fact, I did not pay much attention to the proposed interview because I was very worried that we were still standing in the road and that could expose us to some potential danger. My apprehensions were based on a sensible reason: Raad kept looking around every second, with a watchful, mistrustful eye. More than that, he kept fingering the pistol in its holster, so I guessed that he would have been a target to insurgents. The short time that elapsed before we got into the building seemed like ages, and it reminded me of the horrible time I had passed at the Iraqi border.

The paper was in the second story and consisted of only two small rooms; two writing desks with computers on them were in the first narrow room, while some chairs with simple furniture occupied most of the other room. As we sat in the second room, other committee members slowly filed in.

During the meeting, they were discussing a proposed

play that would be presented to the public in Kurdish.
Because the play had been sponsored by one of the Kurdish parties, the committee had to submit to its
conditions, and so they decided to sprinkle some Arabic
and Turkish words in the text to show the union of Arab,
Turkish, and Kurd nationalities, disregarding the current
violent conflict dominating this oil city. It was not hard to
understand that this ideological propaganda was intended to arrange new conditions in Kirkuk, to help it
later join the Kurdistan region, even though all Arabs and
Turkmens refused this plan. However, this play reminded
me of those silly propaganda schemes operated by Saddam to convince people of the sanctity of his wars despite
the fact that no one believed in their legitimacy. Because I
could not bear to listen to trivialities, I left the meeting
early, blaming Aziz and Ali for their involvement in this
propaganda, but then I considered that they had to earn
their living one way or another.

However, there was another reason to leave the meeting: as I was not a member in the committee, there were
simply not enough chairs at hand.

* * *

It was evening when Ali invited me to have a few beers
at the Doctors' Club. In the past, there had been an exclusive club for artists, where we used to spend the
evenings, but it had been closed for a long time and most
of the artists spent their evenings at the Doctors' Club instead. I couldn't understand why they had chosen this
club because there wasn't any entertainment. Many customers were drinking alcohol in a big garden with lots of
tables and chairs. The management of the club welcomed
everybody, even if they weren't doctors, as long as they
were able to pay. Nothing special happened at that club,
but I had a pleasant time without having to think about
the Islamic bans, the terrorist threat, or even the fear of
the American military forces. I was sure that if I had been
in Baghdad, I wouldn't have been be able to go out for a

drink at night and still return home safely. And from my point of view, this was the biggest difference between Kirkuk and Baghdad. Because it was the first night I had spent outside the house without fear, I was cheering, singing with Ali all the way back home.

But, that feeling didn't last for long. A short time after we arrived at Aziz's home, a big explosion occurred while we were sitting in the hall. It shook everything in the house as if it had penetrated the premises. When we jumped up to investigate, we found that nothing in the house had been damaged, but no one knew what it was and where it had happened because darkness covered everything outside the house. The crowd gathering from the surrounding houses began to speak of a bomb that had blown up an American vehicle on the other side of the soccer field. In the end, no one knew exactly what had happened and soon people began to leave and return to their houses.

In front of Aziz's house, and beside the soccer field, there was a wide space of land on which a big industrial private generator had been set up to supply the surrounding houses with power until 11 p.m. After this time, the dwellers had to rely on the government-supplied power, which was allocated for this suburb only between 2 a.m. and 4 a.m. As a result, we had to spend the 3 hour interval outdoors, because it was too hot and unbearable without the air conditioning on. The government supplied each suburb with a limited amount of electricity per day, and each suburb had been assigned a different connection period, but it would seem that this suburb had been given the worst time. Aziz was always saying that the government meant to punish the suburb where he lived because many attacks against the American military and the local police had occurred there. Wednesday night was the hardest night every week because the blackout on Wednesday night was the longest; it usually started from twelve (midnight) and lasted until 6 a.m. Aziz always argued that the Wednesday night blackouts must have been scheduled by a Kurdish person. Anyhow, he always used to criticize Kurds while he was working within their media, and, from my point of view, I called it hypocrisy.

* * *

Kirkuk: August 10th, 2005

I made up my mind to return to Baghdad and to stay there for a week, thinking that I should give the real estate agent some time to find a buyer. Aziz then requested that I join him on his trip to Arbil, one of the main Kurdish cities in northern Iraq. So I changed my plan. He had to supervise a performance by the Fine Arts school's theatrical group, who were going to compete in a theatrical festival there. As Ali also intended to visit Arbil with his neighbor Hama, I thought it would be a good idea if we all travelled together.

In the morning, Aziz set off for his travel with the theatrical group, and I chose to join him later at Arbil with Ali and Hama. Ali decided to travel in Hama's car instead of his old car. At 8 p.m. that evening we set out on our journey toward the northwest. We passed through some new suburbs under construction at the edge of the old Kirkuk city. This was the land which the Kurdish leadership had granted to the Kurds to encourage them to settle in Kirkuk. While the Kurdish leadership was always proclaiming that their plan was to resettle the Kurds who had been driven out of Kirkuk in Saddam's days, the facts on the ground showed that the numbers of the new settlers were greater than the limited number of Kurds who had left at that time. In any case, if we searched for the real reasons behind all these political tricks, oil would be the answer, because Kirkuk floats on a sea of oil and it is Iraq's second biggest source of oil after the southern oil fields.

Despite the fact that our vehicle was still far away from the oil refineries, we could see the glimmering lights of the gas flares that mark the oil fields. Kirkuk is identified by these lights, which color parts of the dark horizon at nights. Besides these lights, there is the natural gas, which leaks from the ground and burns spontaneously with huge flames once it touches the air. The people call it the 'eternal fire' because it is believed that it was there since the beginning of creation.

We had left Kirkuk behind and yet we had another ninety kilometers to travel before reaching Arbil. No other vehicles were on the road, and the surrounding darkness multiplied my fears for our safety, but I had trust in the self-confidence of Ali and Hama who looked as if they had used this road many times before. I told myself that they wouldn't travel at night unless they were certain that the road was safe. The sight of some glimmering lights from remote villages in the darkness set me free from my fears, and I started enjoying the journey.

I was alone on the back seat while Ali sat next to Hama, who was driving. They were involved in a passionate conversation in Turkmen, the main language used in Kirkuk. I kept watching the road the whole time because I was unable to understand most of the conversation, only a few words and gestures. We passed by Altun Kopri, a Turkmen village thirty kilometers from Kirkuk. I tried my best to make out the features of the village on the left side of the road but I failed because it wasn't moonlit outside. Even the famous old fortress which had always been clearly visible on the right-hand side of the road was completely shrouded in darkness, although it was only a hundred meters away from the road.

I had had to endure a three month stay in this fortress when I was a teacher because, like other teachers, I was obliged to undertake military training in 1987.

The training was held during the long three-month vacation, which was normally given at the end of the school term. This was on Saddam's explicit orders because he wanted to set up militias as a backup for the army during the Iran-Iraq war.

We had been driven to this remote old fortress where the very thick, high walls and the great gates made it very difficult for anybody to escape, or even think of escaping. There, under strict surveillance, we underwent a simple military training program. The place had been deserted for centuries before being reused as a military training center. Thousands of teachers had been waiting anxiously to return to their schools. It was the first time I had ever seen teachers wishing their vacations would finish more quickly; not only because of the hard training but we were afraid that we might all be called up to serve on the front line of the war before the new school year started.

We left the fortress behind and approached the first checkpoint of our trip. When we stopped there, an armed Kurdish man asked us where we had come from and Ali answered him in Kurdish. The armed man swept the car with his eyes and then bent his long body over the car to suspiciously look at our faces before releasing us. Once we had passed through the checkpoint, the view changed completely and the road widened into two lanes divided by a row of trees with modern street-lamps lighting the area. We felt as if we had arrived in another country, leaving Iraq behind, and this sense was proved right when we reached the city. Even though it was 9:30 p.m., the bright shop lights were still attracting the customers and a fun fair on the left side was crowded with families.

It can't be Iraq, I said to myself, thinking that no one could expect to find such a crowd of people at this time of night, in Baghdad, or even in Kirkuk. In fact, Arbil, like many Kurdish cities, had been separated from the central authority of Iraq for a long time.

When Saddam's Army had retaken Kirkuk after the first Gulf War in 1990, the army had stopped at the edge of the Kurdish territories, north of Kirkuk, as if Saddam had set up an undisclosed treaty for a ceasefire between his army and the Kurdish forces. Since then, the Kurdish regions have experienced the best time they've ever had. For about thirteen years, the Kurds had been able to build up their region without Saddam's interference; during this period, they had established a Kurdish government and parliament.

Nothing in this region resembled Iraq; the language, the signs, the customs, and the costumes all bore the stamp of the new Kurdish nation which was forming, away from the mother country, Iraq. The traditional Kurdish flag, which is composed of green, white, and red colors with the sun in the middle, was further evidence of this fact. It was the only flag that we saw and all Kurds felt proud to raise it instead of the traditional Iraqi flag.

Hama drove our vehicle through the busy streets, trying to find the way to a hotel. In front of a big intersection, there was a small neat hotel and Ali chose to spend the night there. But first, we had to obtain permission to stay in Arbil from the police station, according to the regulations of the Kurdish government.

It was a precautionary measure taken for security reasons to observe any strangers coming from outside the region. This procedure had been set up after a pair of radical Muslims blew themselves up on February 1st, 2004 in a crowded place,[8] killing 117 and wounding 260.

I thought that the procedure at the police station would take a long time, but the officer on duty wasn't very meticulous and he only asked us a few questions about the purpose of our visit and where we had come from; soon afterward, he gave us the permits.

We drank some beer and had supper in a large garden belonging to the Kurdish writers' club, which was close to the hotel. At the hotel, we spent a quiet relaxing night in an air-conditioned room, thinking that life must be good in this city where no serious crises could happen, no

---

[8] "Arbil suicide bombers caught on camera." *The Guardian.* 02/04/2004. Michael Howard.

power blackouts, no water shortages, no pollution, and no prohibitions.

* * *

Arbil: August 11th, 2005

Early the next morning, Hama returned to Kirkuk because he had to go to work. I hadn't known this man very long, and I had only had a few short conversations with him during the time that we had spent yesterday at the Kurdish writers club. But even though I couldn't understand the Turkmen language, I was able to uncover the hidden reasons for the favors that he was doing Ali. It wasn't really for free but he had offered to do it in exchange for getting his name registered on the Artists' list, because Kirkuk's council was planning to grant a piece of land to every artist.

I confronted Ali about abusing his position in Kirkuk's Artists' Guild for personal gain, but my remonstrations weren't enough to convince him to stop. On the other hand, he tried to do some good deeds to compensate for his actions, so that he took me with him to visit one of the elder Kurdish artists, giving him some financial aid. This was a gift from the artistic community of Iraq to assist this artist because he was suffering from a chronic disease, and this assignment was the main reason for his trip to Arbil.

Our plan was to find a place to have breakfast before joining my host at the local Theater building. I wasn't able to remember the details of the city because I had only visited it once in my life. A large hill, similar to Uluru rock in central Australia, had been chosen centuries ago to be the centre of the city, while the famous old fortress on the top of this hill was known as one of Arbil's important landmarks.

Arbil's Old City, with its commercial markets, had been built in a circle around this hill, so it was easy to discern our location whenever we looked at the hill. We rested in a traditional small café among the shops, in an old covered market. We sat down on a wooden bench softened by a straw mat, enjoying watching the shops and their customers who wore the traditional embroidered Kurdish costumes. Moreover, I had the good luck to find buffalo cream for breakfast in this café. After we had finished our breakfast, we strolled around in the Old City's markets until 10 a.m. when we were due to meet my host at the local Theater building.

When we got there, the members of the fine arts school's Theater group were practicing on the stage. The auditorium was dark except for the stage, but we were able to find seats. Since the play was in Kurdish, I wasn't able to understand what was going on the stage, but I was still able to evaluate the technical aspects of the acting, as well as the scene design and the direction. After finishing their practice, the group's members began to exchange their points of view, trying to develop their work, and as usual, all the discussion was in Kurdish. The performance time for the play had been changed by the festival's administration, so that it would be presented in the evening instead of the afternoon. Because many groups had to perform their shows on the stage in one day, we thought that it would be better if we went back to Kirkuk early since it wouldn't be easy for us to find public transport to convey us there at night. We left before the show, wishing the group's members a successful performance.

12	**Return to the Troubled City**	

Baghdad: August 13th, 2005

It was 3 p.m. when the minibus, carrying me from Kirkuk, reached its destination at Al-Nahda bus station in Baghdad. Around afternoon, the streets were teeming with people and vehicles, so it was easy to find a public minivan to New-Baghdad. But there I was once again reminded of the horrors lurking in Baghdad's streets, when a large number of American tanks and military vehicles came up Channel Street, obliging all the traffic to move aside. As I watched from the side window of the vehicle, they paraded past proudly while their heads were swiveling over the tanks, looking suspiciously around them, and I thought to myself that all the time I had been in Kirkuk, I had only seen one American vehicle.

Since Sami's wrecker shop was on that street, I asked the minivan driver to drop me there before reaching the destination in New Baghdad. Inside the shop, Sami's forehead was creased with a frown, and he was engaged in some serious discussion with one of his friends. He welcomed me and hastily returned to his friend. I discovered that they were talking about a case that had been referred to the local court, but I wasn't able to figure out what exactly the case was. Soon afterward, a huge, well-built man entered, wearing a traditional Arabic costume. As soon as Sami saw him, he hurried out and greeted him warmly, addressing him as *Sheik*, the title for a clan or religious leader. The Sheik preferred to talk with Sami to one side, while I kept observing, trying to find out who this Sheik was and why he was there.

A few minutes after the Sheik left the place, Sami turned to me and started to tell me about what had happened to him last week. He said that he had arrived home from work one evening to find his neighbor in his house, seizing the opportunity to rob him when nobody was at home. He continued to narrate how, after the burglar had fled, he had informed the local police and the case had been referred to court. But this had only made things worse, for the burglar had begun to threaten him with some armed men belonging to one of the Shia religious Militia, so that he sent his wife, along with their two children, to stay with her sister, in order to keep them away from any trouble.

As for the Sheik, I found out from Sami that he was the head of our clan and he was there on the request of Sami who had asked him for support.

It was the first time I had ever heard about the clan from which I had descended; I had never been concerned about these things in all my life. The same had been true for the rest of my family, but people were now, generally, taking more notice of these social bonds, thinking that membership of large family groups would provide greater protection.

However, the Sheik hadn't offered any assistance except to advise Sami to keep himself out of trouble; maybe this was why he had spoken with him privately, because he didn't want to show others that he had been unable to help.

In fact, the position of the clan head had lost most of its power and authority in Iraqi culture. Agricultural society started to lose its traditional bonds due to the emergence of city life during the fourteenth and fifteenth centuries. The prestige of this role eroded further when Saddam bean to appoint Sheiks based on their loyalty to his regime. Previously, Sheiks had been appointed by a clan council by virtue of their wisdom and capability, but now they were unable to gain the respect of their clan members. And the final "straw that broke the camel's back" was the rise of the religious leaders as great powers, which weakened the Sheiks' role even further. For these reasons, no one paid much attention to the Sheik's appearance, except Sami whom I thought to be unwise for relying on a person who had long lost his authority.

While I was admonishing Sami to cease the proceedings in the court in order to avoid any troubles, he revealed that another problem had happened in my absence. An awful incident took place opposite the workshop a few days ago. A private car drew up by the edge of the road, about twenty meters from Sami's garage, where a sheepherder sold sheep every day. A man got out from the car to buy a sheep. Just then, another vehicle stopped there, suddenly; some armed men dismounted and shot the buyer in cold blood; then they got in their car and drove off.

In a shaking voice, Sami described the victim's blood as a splashing fountain that stained the sheepherder who fled, never to return. Despite having fought in the Iraq-Iran war for several years, during compulsory military service, and having seen a lot of violence and bloodshed in battles, Sami had been shocked by the scene. He bent his head and sighed, his face looking pale. He was worried of getting involved in an interrogation about that unknown victim although the police hadn't questioned him yet, but he was anxious about the coming days.

"Why are you worried? Even if they ask you, just tell them what you had seen," I commented.

"Problems come one after the other, only if this sheepherder gets back to his job, he was a witness," Sami said gloomily.

"A lot of these incidents happen every day; many bodies are thrown away on the streets and no one asks who and why! Don't overstate your case," said Sami's friend, who stood close, indifferently.

With downcast eyes, he said a few words regarding this subject, mentioning his longing to leave Iraq, pausing with a sigh. But what would be the consequences after leaving? Many people have tried this before and failed; they sold all their property and traveled to the surrounding Arab countries to face other kinds of hardship, encountering poverty, risks, and swindlers. They strived, struggled to endure, lined up every day before the offices of the UN High Commissioner on Refugees (UNHCR), and tried to contact any relative dwelling overseas to give them a hand. But in the end, most of them failed and, after spending all they had, returned to Iraq with their disappointment trailing behind.

Sami might have borne in his mind all these difficulties, yet he did not utter a word about them. I had discussed these things with him many times before, and my opinion had always been that he must lighten his burden, because he put all his cash in auto-wrecks and these things could not be sold in a month, or even in a year. He took some practical steps when he already sold somebody's auto-wrecks in bulk, but still had plenty of parts strewn all about the garage.

* * *

New Baghdad: August 14th, 2005

At my sister's home, everything was the same as before; but in the evening, a dark cloud spread over our heads when my young brother Mohamed arrived to report that some unknown men were chasing him in a black vehicle. He said that they had followed him to his shop (he made car seat covers), trying to catch him alone, but he had been able to slip away and merge into a crowd of people. Once she heard this news, my mother yelled in terror, telling him that he shouldn't go to his shop again. We were all taken aback as we guessed that those men who had chased him were from one of the Shia militia's assassination gangs. This was the first time that the assassination gang "ghosts" we had only heard about had threatened one of the family.

All the family blamed him because of his constant diatribes against the Shias. Even Sami, whom I had thought would be on his side, criticized him, demanding that he cease his reckless behavior for the sake of his children. However, nothing could uproot those dark ideas from his mind or quell his fanaticism, and he persisted in proclaiming his enmity towards the Shias and his determination to proclaim what he called "God's will," wherever and whenever he was, regardless of the consequences.

With all the troubles that surrounded me since the moment I had arrived in Baghdad, I made up my mind to return to Kirkuk the next day. In the meantime, Sami asked me to spend the night with him at his home as he now had to stay by himself. Even though I knew he would seize the opportunity to drag me into the pointless religious discussions, I accepted his invitation because he insisted. Besides, I thought that it would be easy to catch a van to Al-Nahda central bus station in the early morning for his house was very close to New Baghdad's main street in which many vans were available.

The smell of the air inside the old half-brick house, where Sami dwelled, was thick with humidity since the sunlight rarely reached the dark rooms. Some spare car parts were strewn about the front yard, which was covered by a pool of stagnant water from a constantly leaking, rusty air conditioner outside the front window. Although he owned a better house, Sami preferred to rent this small one because it was close to his garage. However, after the previous quarrel with his neighbor, he had begun to think of searching for another house to live in.

As I had expected, after a short time, Sami turned his computer on, and started playing the DVD of the Islamic preacher, Ahmed Deedat, which he had already attempted to play in my next eldest brother's house.

His house still had power as most of the street's houses were supplied by an industrial generator set up on the footpath of a back street.

I lay on a couch with the computer behind me, but I could still hear the voice of the Islamic preacher plagiarizing some verses from the Bible, trying to find any fissures in the text that might enable him to disprove it.

I felt it was a sort of torture to force me to listen to something I didn't want to. It wasn't the first time Sami had done it. At my sister's home, when my brothers and I gathered almost every night, he used to select an Islamic TV Channel and turn up the volume as if he wanted to thrust the Qur'anic verses into my mind. I always thought that I should be patient and able to absorb the pressure because I already knew that Sami did all these things with love, thinking he was trying to save my soul, as he believed.

The DVD was playing a debate in an American church between Ahmed Deedat and an American pastor, who was defending the Bible. One of the important issues Deedat was disputing was whether Jesus really died on the cross. Muslims dispute whether this really happened, believing that the person who died on the cross wasn't Jesus. Ahmed Deedat cited what Jesus mentioned about his fate that he must be inside the grave for three days like Jonah who stayed inside the fish for three days and three nights. Thus, Deedat asserted that Jesus was alive in the grave according to his interpretation, because Jonah was alive too.

I was listening without saying a word, but it was obvious that Deedat had already chosen the breaks and was darting briskly through them, before his opponent could guess which point his adversary was going to dispute, and this gave Deedat an advantage. In the last part of the debate, the American preacher regained his footing somewhat, so that he was able to land some punches, but he was still on the defensive.

Silently, I lay on the couch, praying to God with closed eyes, to give Sami some words to touch his heart. I knew whatever I said wouldn't be effective without God intervening. Soon after, I heard a clear message when the pastor began to explain the meaning of the forgiveness of God; he said that a Muslim man couldn't show any leniency toward his daughter if she fell into sin, and he must punish her. He explained how, in the same way, God cannot ignore the sin of mankind, and he must punish. But in his mercy, he put the punishment on his son so that we could have forgiveness.

When the debate finished, Sami took the DVD very carefully to put it back inside its cover; then he turned off the computer. I had seen thousands of copies of this DVD, sold by peddlers in the crowded streets of Baghdad, which shows the general antagonism towards Christianity. I was able to notice that this hostile spirit was a weird guest in the Iraqi community, and it had emerged only after the invasion of Iraq, which provoked and antagonized radical Islam.

Sami tried to drag me into an argument but I did my best to avoid it, because I already knew that there could be no winner or loser. Eventually, I broke my silence, telling him that without reading the Bible, he couldn't discuss these things and he mustn't rely on this preacher or on anyone else, but he must find out for himself, because Deedat was distorting the meaning of the Bible verse.

"It was a figure of speech when Jesus said he was like Jonah; that doesn't mean he didn't die on the cross. It's just like the Qur'anic verse that says that God sat down on his throne. That doesn't mean God literally has a chair to sit on. Besides, there are many verses in which Jesus declared obviously that death would claim him. You should read the Bible by yourself to find out the reason why Jesus used this aphorism, and on what occasion." I explained this to him politely, trying to keep myself cool.

"I am not empowered yet to read the Bible," Sami replied.

"What do you mean when you say you are not empowered? Who would empower you?" I said sharply.

"Namely... I can't read it, the Bible is not my book. I am not eligible to do so," he said uncertainly.

"But you must read everything; you can't live like a horse with blinders."

"The Bible is distorted," he said, just like all typical Muslims.

"OK, show me the distorted parts. You should read the Bible first to find out if it's been distorted. If I told you I had a dollar, how could you know whether it's counterfeit or legitimate; you would have to touch it and feel it with your fingers; then you could decide," I argued. But he preferred to be evasive.

"The Bible consists of many things against my creed; I can't accept them," he said, trying to make an excuse.

"Like what?"

"Biographical things; it insults some prophets. Take the story of King David, for instance; the Bible says that David was an adulterer!"

"But the Qur'an mentions that Moses killed the Egyptian! Yet you accept it!"

"Yes, Moses killed, but the Qur'an didn't say he was an adulterer," he replied doubtfully.

"This is a cultural misunderstanding. As an Arab, you can accept somebody to be a killer but not an adulterer! The fact is that all mankind are sinners, and no one is perfect but God; this is what the Bible is trying to say."

If we hadn't been interrupted by a blackout, we could have gone on for a long time. And so, when the operator of the generator switched the power off at 11 p.m., I seized the opportunity to end the discussion, closing my eyes to sleep.

13 | Unexpected Difficulties

Kirkuk: August 15th, 2005

When I arrived in Kirkuk the next afternoon, the first thing I intended to do was to contact Aziz. Since there were no public phones, I walked down to the city center, toward the Department of Communications, as this was the only place where I could make a call. I was strolling cheerfully along, thinking that I had left my troubles behind in Baghdad. But it seemed that trouble was following me, even in Kirkuk. When I dialed Aziz, I heard the voice of his wife on the other end, telling me that Ali had informed her that my unfinished house had been sold.

I hurried to meet Ali at his home, where he explained that when he had gone to see the house, a neighbor had told him that my house had been purchased. A relative of a Kurdish man living near my property claimed that he had already bought it from the owner, which wasn't me.

Ali said he had discussed the matter with this Kurdish dweller, demanding some proof of purchase. But the Kurdish man had been uncooperative and quite aggressive. Ali was a very reliable person; he didn't delay but immediately drove me to my property. I was thinking that if somebody was claiming ownership of the house, he wouldn't be able to prove it, because I had already made certain that I was the only registered owner.

The neighbor, whose son inhabited my house, was a devious man. I had realized this from the moment I met him.

"I have checked the registration records. I am the only one who owns the house," I assured him.

"I don't want to involve myself in any trouble. I want to keep out of this," he said, pretending neutrality. He said that the buyer worked in the governor's office, part of internal security. His rank of *Nakeeb* was equal to a sergeant in the military. After telling me this, he brought a small piece of paper with the buyer's mobile number. It was clear that somebody was working to swindle me and the neighbor had connived with him.

Ali suggested we contact Abdullah (the lawyer) for legal advice. In the afternoon, Abdullah received me and Ali at his home. He confirmed what I had already guessed: that somebody was working to swindle me. But he asserted that I was the sole owner according to the records and nobody could change this fact. However, his assuring and confident manner wasn't enough to bring relief to me, because I already knew that supremacy in Iraq lay with force rather than law. Even though he professed his certainty, he still suggested asking a Kurdish acquaintance of his who also worked as a sergeant (*Nakeeb*) in the governor's office. Without delay, he made a call to him on his mobile phone, and the answer from other end of the line was clear and immediate; no one of that name worked as an officer in internal security. The Kurdish sergeant, whose name was Nozad, promised to call the buyer immediately to be certain of his allegations. Soon afterward, Abdullah received a call back. Nozad informed him that the buyer had denied the allegation that he worked in the governor's office, but he didn't deny purchasing the house. A meeting was arranged for the next week to solve the problem.

The feeling of delight which had filled me since the moment I had found my house turned into disappointment as I realized that selling the property wouldn't be easy. Even though the real estate agent referred many customers to inspect the house, the neighbor warned them about the uncertain ownership, so no one was disposed to purchase it or to get into any trouble. The real estate agent advised me to evict the Arabic neighbor's son, but I thought that an empty house would be easy prey for Kurdish squatters, and so the problem would become worse than ever, because the Kurds were influential in Kirkuk and nobody could force them to leave.

A few days later, Abdullah informed me that he would come with Nakeeb Nozad that afternoon to Ali's house, and then we would travel together to meet the person who had claimed to have purchased the property. The picture I had built up in my mind of Nozad was foggy, but I had imagined that he would be a huge man in his forties with a big moustache like most Kurds. But my imagination proved wrong. He was about twenty-five and of an average height. Besides, he had no moustache. I thought to myself that if anyone had wanted to be a Nakeeb in Saddam's days, he would have needed to spend four years in training at the Police Academy, followed by ten years of working as a junior officer. It would seem that the procedures of the Kurdish force were much more easygoing because it could be easy for anyone to be a sergeant, or even a major, in a few years. Nozad wore civilian clothes and talked in such a confident manner that he could persuade anyone that he was capable of solving any problem.

Abdullah, together with Nozad, instructed Ali to follow them. So, I traveled in Ali's car, while Abdullah, Nozad, and another young Kurdish man drove ahead of us in their modern vehicle.

Our cars headed toward the western side of Kirkuk where the meeting would be held, in Arafa, the suburb where most of the oil industry was located. Before reaching the suburb's main street, Nozad stopped his car by the side of the road, and so Ali parked nearby. When I got out of the car to enquire about why they had stopped, Nozad was standing beside his vehicle making a call on his mobile. Eventually, I came to understand that there was no specific place to meet and they were receiving directions over the phone. Soon afterward, we set off again toward Arafa, and their vehicle turned left to take the road leading away from the inhabited urban suburb toward the industrial complexes.

Since it was a remote area, I sensed that unpleasant events were awaiting us, and so I began to wish that I hadn't come on this unpredictable errand. When we reached the oil police checkpoint, we parked our vehicles in the car park to the side because we were unable to drive any further. Nozad got out of his car while listening to the instructions on his mobile phone. Eventually, he turned off his mobile and asked us to follow him. We did so, toward a small one-storey brick building at the checkpoint, where an armed man in Kurdish traditional costume stood beside the barriers. When the armed man stopped us he began talking in Kurdish, and in turn, Nozad answered him. Then Nozad turned to me and asked me to go with him but also that the others must wait outside. Abdullah protested that he should stay with me as he was my lawyer, but the armed man was very strict with his instructions.

I followed Nozad up the few steps into the building. We met some other armed men in the hallway, and one of them led us into an office. In there, I found three men in Kurdish costume sitting on seats while a stout man in army uniform sat behind a large office desk. A tall, thin young man took his seat beside the office desk and I guessed that he was the buyer because his casual dress set him apart from the others. As soon we sat down, a conversation began in Kurdish between the stout man behind the desk and Nozad. I was concentrating on trying to decipher the meaning from their gestures and body language. The man in front of me was squatting on his seat in his wide dark Kurdish pants. His large moustache gave him a stern appearance, and he spent the whole time gazing at me aggressively.

The conversation was entirely in Kurdish and it took a long time, so I stopped trying to follow it. But finally, the stout man addressed me, in poor Arabic, telling me that the buyer had purchased the house legally because there was indeed another person who owned the house. And he tried to explain that many properties had been given to other people by Saddam's regime.

"OK, can he show me any papers or documents to prove that there is another owner?" I replied.

But the tall thin man began to explain in Kurdish. While they continued in Kurdish, I thought to myself that this meeting was held in this remote place and with these armed men, just to frighten me with a demonstration of power. The conversation didn't turn to Arabic again, and after a while, Nozad rose up, and so did the other men. I understood that it was the end of the meeting. When we got out of the building, the others were waiting worriedly and they asked Nozad about what happened, but he didn't want to talk till we reached the car park.

"Look, those people persisted in claiming the house, but they have no documents and no papers," Nozad said, explaining that the buyer now denied that he had purchased the house for himself, and referred us back once again to his relative, who lived next to my unfinished property.

Nozad advised us to go straightaway to meet that person, so we turned around and traveled in the opposite direction, toward my property.

On the way, I thought about everything that had happened, realizing that a trap was being set for me. When we reached the place, Nozad made a decision that I mustn't talk directly to my Kurdish neighbors, so I stayed in the car with Ali, at a distance from them. When Abdullah and Nozad spent a long time negotiating with my neighbor, I began to contemplate what was going on around me. I hadn't been satisfied with the quick choices

of Nozad, starting with his consenting to go to that remote place where the meeting was held. All the way, he
had been displaying immature behavior and making im-
pulsive decisions.

When he came back with Abdullah, the confident image that he had been presenting to us began to crack and
the confident voice had now become an uncertain tone.
He said that the Kurdish neighbor was a violent person
and he was talking with a gun in his hand, threatening
that if anyone approached the property, he would put a
bullet in his head. As they were talking, I made up my
mind to give up on selling the house, thinking it wasn't
worth the trouble as the highest price had been paid by
the real estate was about twenty million Iraqi Dinars,
equal to $20,000.

But this was neither Abdullah's opinion nor that of Nozad, and they kept coming up with ideas to protect my
rights. One of these queer suggestions was to transfer the
ownership of the house to one of them. Their argument
was that it would prevent my Kurdish neighbor from re-
gistering the house in his name. It was obvious that their
justifications were silly and unbelievable, because if my
neighbor had been able to transfer the possession easily,
he would have done so years ago. Something inside me
said, "This is a con." And I began to think that some of
the things that were happening were suspicious. I asked
myself why Nozad had insisted on keeping me from talking directly with my Kurdish neighbor, and whether this
neighbor had really been holding a gun when he talked
with them. Actually, I couldn't see them when they were
negotiating because the car was parked far away; even
during the meeting in that remote place, I hadn't been
able to understand what they had talked about because
all the conversation had been in Kurdish. The repeated
demands of Abdullah and Nozad reinforced my suspicions, so I decided to be very cautious.

One of Abdullah's propositions was that we should notify the property registrar that somebody was trying to seize the property, as a safety procedure. They kept referring to the registrar by his first name, as if he were one of their acquaintances. At any rate, I thought that this would be harmless, and so I consented to meet Abdullah the next morning at the registration office.

The registration office was on the third level of the local court building, but before one could get inside, a thorough search was conducted at the main gate. The place was crammed with people and the ground floor was drawing people in from outside and pumping them into upper levels. Since there was only one elevator, and it would be a long wait, I headed toward the stairs. A flood of people surged upward and carried me with them, depositing me on the third floor. This was so crowded that I wondered how I would find Abdullah among all those people. I took up a position at the top of the stairs, thinking that I would be able to meet him when he came, but after a few minutes, he arrived from another direction. He asked me to wait for Nozad and as we waited, he began to draw up a petition on a sheet of paper requesting to renew my ownership papers, saying that if we got new documents that would be a convincing proof of my possession. When Nozad came, we went into the registrar's office. The room was small, and so filled with claimants that we could hardly find a place to stand. The registrar sat behind a large table and I noticed that he was looking at Abdullah and Nozad as if he hadn't seen them before. Eventually, our turn came, and Abdullah handed him my petition, but the registrar looked at him with contempt. "What do you want?" he said to Abdullah, who looked befuddled and explained our problem, in a trembling voice.

"Who is the owner?" the registrar asked.

"I am" I replied.

"Have you got authorization to act on behalf of your client?" the registrar asked Abdullah in a firmer voice.

"The client is my relative," Abdullah responded timorously but the registrar told him to leave the room because he was not authorized to represent me.

"And you, what do you want?" the registrar addressed Nozad.

"I'm with them, Nakeeb Nozad," Nozad introduced himself, but the registrar told him to leave the room also. When they had both left, I handed over the petition by myself and the registrar wrote his consent on it. Outside, Nozad and Abdullah seemed very frustrated. And the superior and confident image they had always tried to project was melting away. After Nozad left the place, it occurred to me that he might not have really been a sergeant after all, and that perhaps even Abdullah, who now chose to withdraw, might have been an apprentice.

No one could enter the filing room, and the only way to hand over a petition was to queue up outside a small window. Two meters from the window, on the left side, was another small window reserved for lawyers. Because many clients were already in the queue, and I was the last one, I spent more than one hour waiting to hand over my papers while the clients would often try to jump the queue, shouting and scrambling over each other.

Finally, my turn came and I was able to reach the window. I gave my petition to the file manager, who was responsible for all the property records in Kirkuk. He was flustered and sweating from having had to cope with all these impatient claimants. When he read my petition, he looked at me in astonishment, and said, "You came all the way from Australia to claim this property? What is wrong with you?"

"No, I just came to visit my friends and found my property," I explained while he continued reading my file.

"Twelve years! And you expect the property to still be in your name!" He laughed, because everybody knew that most deserted units in the area had been given away to other people by the previous regime. But when he opened my property file, he started to nod approvingly.

"Yes, it is still in your name; it must be a miracle," he said.

"But it is an unfinished miracle, because many greedy people are trying grab it," I added, but he confirmed that nobody could take it without my consent. When he gave me the new possession papers, he repeated that no sale could take place unless I came into his office and gave permission in person.

"Can I swap it for one in another suburb?" I asked him.

"No you can't, because your papers show that you are from Baghdad and you're not allowed to buy property in Kirkuk, but you can sell your current property," he stated firmly.

When I left the building, the man's voice still echoed in my mind, and I was disappointed to have confirmed that I couldn't buy a house in Kirkuk. It was the same as the policy under Saddam's regime that prohibited Kurds from buying real estate in Kirkuk, but now the process had been reversed. When I saw Ali, he assured me that this was the case, explaining that if I sold my property, it would take three weeks to register the contract and all the papers would have to be sent to the governor's office so that the buyer's background could be verified. Only then would the governor allow the sale.

14 | Time to Leave

Baghdad: August 19th, 2005

When Ali decided to travel to Syria, I thought it would be the perfect time to join him and leave Iraq behind. I had considered many times what would be the safest way to depart from all this chaos around me, but I always deferred setting out because of my previous experience on the road from Baghdad to Amman. Getting a flight to Amman wasn't simple either, because of the extremely high demand for tickets. Besides that, the high insurance premiums had led to grossly inflated prices.

"Yes, that's a great idea," I responded enthusiastically, when my friend revealed his desire to travel to Syria on the northwestern road from Mosul city. This road was much safer than the road to Amman and many cities and towns lay along the way.

Because of the lack of security in Iraq, most Iraqi artists had moved to Syria to shoot their TV shows, and my friend thought that he might be able to get a part in one of their soap operas. We arranged to start our trip the next week, thinking that selling my property could be done when circumstances improved, despite the fact that I continued feeling pessimistic about any possible improvement during the coming years. But before we set off to Syria, I had to travel to Baghdad, first; not only to say goodbye to my family, but also because my luggage was still at my sister's house.

It was five in the afternoon when I reached Al-Nahda bus station in Baghdad. Public transport was scarce at that particular time, and there were only a couple of taxis parked beside the main gate. I was unwilling to hire a taxi, but I had no other choice. The atmosphere during the trip was tense and the untidy dress of the tall slim driver gave me the impression that he was not to be trusted. On the highway, the traffic was much busier as if all the drivers were racing to reach their homes before dark. Two vehicles were actually racing, zigzagging recklessly and confusing the traffic. Unfortunately, our car ended up between them. At first, I thought it was just some sort of foolish competition between two young drivers, but it turned out to be more serious when a man in one of the vehicles aimed a pistol toward the other vehicle, which was moving parallel to our car. Since our car was in the middle, the pistol was pointing directly at my face for some time. I screamed for the driver to slow down, and so he let the vehicles overtake our car and disappear into the traffic.

These horrible moments made me determined to leave Iraq in any possible way, thinking that every day in Baghdad would be worse than the previous one. The driver disliked driving me to my sister's house and he decided to drop me in New Baghdad instead. He said that it was unsafe to go any further. When I got out, it was dark and people were hurrying to the public transport stop. Some of those minibuses were still parked by the main street and I was able to get a seat in one, which took me to my sister's house.

When I told my mother about my decision to leave Iraq, she grieved because she had thought I would stay much longer, but after a while she realized that I would have to leave sooner or later. The next evening, the TV news bulletin drew our attention to a terrible explosion that had happened at Al-Nahda bus station; 43 people had been killed and 89 injured[9]. The incident had occurred in the early evening when a vehicle loaded with dynamite ex-

---

[9] "Bombs kill 43 in Iraq." *Indiana Gazette*. 08/17/2005, p. 10.

ploded. *I could easily have been one of the victims, if I had arrived in Al-Nahdah today,* I thought.

I always thought that God would take care of me and protect me in the midst of these incidents. While I was looking at the images of bombed vehicles on the news, my hand slid into my pocket and touched a small piece of folded paper. On this, I had written Psalm ninety one and this was always with me. I used to repeat some parts of it to myself from time to time:

> *Do not be afraid of the terrors of the night, Nor fear the danger of the day, Nor dread the plague that stalks in darkness, Nor the disaster that strikes at midday, though a thousand fall at your side, Though ten thousand are dying around you, these evils will not touch you.*

Salim advised me to delay my travel to Kirkuk because no buses could enter Al-Nahda bus station as a result of the destruction. But despite his advice, I insisted travelling the next morning, whatever the difficulties. I made a quick visit to my brother Hisham to bid farewell, while I called the other brothers and relatives by telephone.

* * *

Baghdad: August 21st, 2005

In the morning, Salim was ready to give me a lift to Al-Nahda bus station. I didn't encourage my mother to accompany me, although she would have liked to, but she suggested going with me just as far as the center of New Baghdad, since she wanted to go to the vegetable market.

In New-Baghdad, the streets were jammed with cars and people. Salim was doing his best to find a place to drop my mother at the market, and finally he managed to squeeze his car into a line of parked vehicles on the side of the road to let my mother get out. Before we left her behind, she bent her head through the right hand window and kissed me with tears running down her cheeks.

The way from New Baghdad to Al-Nahda was very difficult. One of the entrances to the freeway was nearly blocked, with vehicles crawling very slowly. When we got further along, we found out that the reason for the delay was a long queue of vehicles waiting to fill up at a nearby gas station and it extended a whole kilometer, obstructing access to the freeway. When we approached Al-Nahda bus station, the traffic turned out to be much heavier than before. I thought that all circumstances were conspiring to prevent me from leaving Baghdad. But my obstinate desire to wake up from this nightmare was much stronger than any obstacles.

At the intersection fifty meters from Al-Nahda bus station, the streets were completely blocked with barriers and police vehicles, so Salim couldn't go any further. He dropped me there with my heavy luggage, and then quickly turned back because, at that moment, a big explosion occurred somewhere in Baghdad's center, shaking everything around us, and sending the frightened traffic into chaos.

I could barely drag my luggage, hoping to find a minivan to Kirkuk, but when I reached the main gate of the bus station, it was closed. A big black patch of soot pointed to yesterday's great explosion and was clearly visible on the cracked gateposts. Beyond the gate, the sight was not much better for plenty of vehicles and buses had been charred by the impact of the blast. Some station employees were leading passengers, including me, to an adjacent fenced area that was being used instead of the old station. Inside the substitute station, there was only one bus, ready to set off for Basra, the main city of southern Iraq, and meanwhile the few other passengers stood near their luggage, waiting for any bus to come and carry them.

The ground was bare except for some scraps of iron from the destroyed vehicles. The wind carried a curious odor; I guessed it was the smell of the charred vehicles, as well as corpses. A long time passed but no bus ventured into the place. Finally, I dragged my luggage again and left the fenced area to see if I could find any transportation to Kirkuk. Within a short distance, I found a minivan going to Kirkuk, so I hurried to load my luggage and take my seat. I felt relieved to have dropped my heavy luggage.

I kept looking at the people and vehicles around me through the side window, anticipating that an explosion might happen any time. Everything was in a mess as cars and buses turned the sidewalks into parking spaces, obstructing the pedestrians from walking. I was the only passenger in the vehicle and the driver was yelling to draw attention to his destination.

"Kirkuk... Kirkuk... Kirkuk" he kept yelling with all the force of his lungs, but no one seemed interested in going to Kirkuk.

I am stuck in Baghdad, a horrible voice rang in my head, snatching away my peace and calmness. My head starting turning side-to-side, as if I were a rat caught in a trap.

"Kirkuk... Kirkuk..." the driver continued to shout in vain.

I felt like Virata, from the Hindu epic *Mahabharata,* in the book's final act. This story was still stuck in my mind even though I had read it many years ago. There was an Arabic translation and I always dreamt to adapt it to theater. Virata was a warrior in ancient India, who, in the heat of battle, discovered his own humanity and chose to abandon the battlefields to become a judge. As a seeker of truth, he made a vital decision when he defied a prisoner who accused him of injustice. He struck a deal with the prisoner to substitute for him for a period of time in order to learn about life in prison. They swapped their garments so the prisoner escaped confinement my disguising himself as the judge, meanwhile Virata remained in the prison.

Virata stayed calm for many days, enduring the rough

life in small low-roofed dungeon, thinking that perhaps life could still be bearable even in a place like this. Before the time was due for the prisoner to return back, a terrible idea struck him and drained all his acquired stillness and tranquillity.

"What if the prisoner never came back?" this question could have driven him to madness, especially when he lost the ability to count days, hours and minutes. As a result, this period seemed like an eternity, and only within these moments he felt really what life was like in prison.

"Kirkuk... Kirkuk..." played in my head like a drumbeat, and the few minutes I spent waiting felt like an eternity as well.

Bitterly, I realized that all the time I had spent in Baghdad was just like Virata before his disturbing thought. Believing that I had a chance to get out of Iraq gave my soul a sense of serenity. Soon afterward, I thought of the American soldiers and foreigners who worked and served in Iraq. Through all perilous events that they confronted every day, they still knew that they would leave this burning land and return to their cosy homes. Surely this hope gave them some peace of mind to overcome the hardships of living in Iraq. Some American soldiers lost this glimmer of hope, and perhaps their traumas drove them to lose their psychological balance and in some cases commit suicide.

The driver walked across to the other side of the street, looking for any passengers and this multiplied my fears. I was alone in the van, turning my head back and forth; gazing at the confounded people in the street. Everyone casted about looking for buses or vans. Meantime, sirens of police vehicles worsened the disturbance.

What was my reason for my trip to Iraq? I asked myself. Was it to share my brother his ordeal for losing his son? Or there was another reason that could be added to my excuses? Maybe I attempted to discover my own humanity as a seeker of truth as Virata did before, I reflected.

Ruminating on all these things I flagged down an Iraqi actress whom I had met in Jordan before my trip to Iraq. At that time, I was hesitant and unable to commit to either travelling to Iraq or returning to Australia. Coincidentally, she had just returned from Baghdad at that time and of course I asked her, "How is life in Iraq?"

"You should go yourself to see what is happening," she replied bitterly, unable to conceal the implied reprimand.

The confident way she talked to me spurred my courage and it broke the deadlock. Did she accuse me of disloyalty to my mother country just because I had chosen to leave? Maybe. Quite possibly my trip to Iraq during this difficult time was an effort to defy her concealed accusation. Anyhow, I now wished I had not listened to her advice.

I looked around me, but although the driver was still hidden from my sight, I felt much better when I started to think realistically about the alternatives that were still open. For example, I could return back to my sister's home and arrange another plan to join Ali in Kirkuk.

Anyway, I did not have to do all these things because the driver returned in a hurry to tell me that across the street there were lots of minivans going to Kirkuk, and he was going to park with them.

"Stay in the van, I will take you there!" he said while he pulled van out quickly, making a wide turn to the other side of the street. I exhaled loudly in relief, setting aside all the black thoughts for the moment.

The opposite sidewalk was occupied by a line of vehicles, which my driver joined. As soon as he parked in the queue, he told me that I was free to change vehicles; so I carried my luggage again to the minivan at the head of the queue. This van was nearly full, and most of the passengers were Kurds. Soon afterward, the last passenger took the last seat available, and the van set out immediately for Kirkuk. As soon as the vehicle began to move, another explosion occurred somewhere, and when the van had climbed up the eight-meter hill to the highway, I was able to see the smoke of the explosions. They were making thick black clouds and releasing them to the wind, as if the grieving city was bidding me farewell.

* * *

15 | Out of Context

After I left Iraq, circumstances got worse, especially in 2006, which was considered the worst violent year. That year, the number of corpses flung on the streets grew steadily; many of them were unrecognizable because of the torture they had been put through. Fingers pointed at the militias and some gangs called "the death squads".

Since the invasion of Iraq, the serial murders of scientists and intellectuals never stopped and, as usual, there were no investigations and inquiries about the identities; they were always registered as "unknown".

Reports issued from the Ministry of Higher Education and Scientific Research confirmed that the assassination of more than 250 university lecturers had occurred, but they neglected to count the employees of private universities.

The Ministry of Health also announced that 121 registered physicians had been killed since the entry of the occupying forces in Iraq. And as before, this official figure did not include doctors who worked in private hospitals or who left the country after being subjected to threats.

Study in universities was being repeatedly stopped due to the danger of exposing teachers as targets, while the Iraqi collective memory still bore the kidnapping incident of about 150 academics in front of the department of Service Missions[10] (part of the Ministry of Education) in November 2006.

---

[10] "Scores of academics seized in mass kidnap." *The Guardian.* 11/15/2006, p. 4.

Even the government became complicit in this chaos when the ascendant Shia parties merged their militias into the police and army, which then drifted further from their impartiality. Political observers announced through different Arabic media that Iranians had succeeded in infiltrating into Iraqi forces in a legal way because of the strong alliance between these militias and Iran. Effectively, issues such as liquidation of opponents and taking revenge on high ranking Iraqi officers, who had participated in Saddam's war against Iran, became routine.

The mass graves, which have been used by international society as evidence of Saddam's crimes, have emerged anew as many new unmarked gravesites have been discovered recently. There is no way to name the persons or groups who were originally behind these crimes.

On the other hand, nobody can stop the frequent explosions caused by car bombs, explosive booby-traps, and the flying mortar bombs despite all defensive attempts by the Iraqi government during the last three years.

Before he left his position as the Secretary General of the UN, Kofi Annan declared in a BBC interview that the level of violence in Iraq was "much worse" than that of Lebanon's civil war. He added, "A few years ago, when we had the strife in Lebanon and other places, we called that a civil war; this is much worse." Also, he said that, "Although Saddam Hussein had been a brutal dictator, at least there had been peace in the streets and people were secure in their everyday lives. The life for the ordinary Iraqi is now much worse than it was before the war." That was Annan's declaration on the 4th of December, 2006.

On Friday, September 14, 2007, Opinion Research Business (ORB), an independent polling agency located in London, published estimates of the total war casualties in Iraq since the US-led invasion of Iraq in 2003. Standing at over 1.2 million deaths (1,220,580), this estimate is not the highest number as it continued to climb in subsequent years.

My cousin Wahab, whom I met in Sami's workshop, was one of these victims. Though there was no proof of his death yet, his family lost any hope of finding him alive after an armed Shia group captured him at his home a while after my departure from Iraq.

Raad Mutasha Al-Issawi, the editor-in-chief of *Al-Raad*, the local paper in Kirkuk, also faced the same fate, but in a different way. He was assassinated on May 9th, 2007 in a car along with three of his colleagues by insurgents who opened fire with machine guns from another vehicle.[11]

Besides the interference of Iran in Iraq, specialists in Iraqi issues gave another reason underlying the instability and the constant violence –the stumbling politics based on wrong foundations from the beginnings of the dramatic changes in Iraq in 2003. They mentioned the crucial decision of Mr. L. Paul Bremer, the U.S. administrator of Iraq, who had dissolved Iraq's 500,000-member military and intelligence services and outlawed the Baath Party (Saddam's party), and dismissed all senior members from their government posts.

Bremer's policy of *debaathification* (the expression used for banning Baathists) excluded thousands of experienced government workers, some of whom may not have committed crimes during the former regime, from playing a role in the new Iraq, and this decision was and is still the main obstacle, which has been preventing political reconciliation between foes. Anyway, Mr. Bremer and other U.S officials realized their fault early on and began to shift their strategy. Consequently, and in a bid to strengthen the officer corps, they allowed some senior ex-Baathists to return to the security forces. Baathists "who do not have blood on their hands" and who were "innocent and competent" could play a role in Iraq's reconstruction, coa-

---

[11] "Suicide bomb strikes peaceful Kurdish city in Iraq", *USA Today*. May 9th, 2007. Also, www.newssafety.org posting.

lition spokesman Dan Senor announced on April 24, 2004.

Bremer had announced in the same month that the debaathification had been "poorly implemented" and applied "unevenly and unjustly", and said he supported a plan to allow "vetted senior officers from the former regime" back into the military services, and this would accelerate the formation of Iraq's security forces because Iraq's police and military were largely unable to stand up to the increasingly aggressive insurgents.

Two months later, Bremer dissolved the Supreme National Debaathification Commission, but the panel continued to operate by a different name, which was "Accountability and Justice Commission

It was obvious that Iran would not like to fold its papers with Saddam's regime, pushing its loyal Shia parties to reject any political settlement.

Interim Prime Minister Ayad Allawi, who had headed the first temporary government in June 2004, continued the policy of the reconciliation as he backed the return of vetted ex-Baathists to the security services, but the elected Shia coalition governments, who came after Allawi, ignored this course and considered it as if it was some sort of compensation for people who already hand-in-hand with Saddam. Many observers believed that Shia coalition governments could have achieved a lot of progress if they had shown forgiveness to people who had not been involved in crimes.

Unlike Allawi, these governments went in the opposite direction, especially the police and military forces, when some ascendant Shia parties merged their militias into the police and military forces, which then drifted further from their impartiality. Political observers announced through different Arabic media that Iran succeeded in slipping into the Iraqi forces in a legal way because of the strong alliance between these militias and Iran. Effectively, issues such as liquidation of opponents and taking revenge on Iraqi high rank officers, who had participated in Saddam's war against Iran, became very easy assignment.

Thus, the government became one of the main factors of the chaos in Iraq. On the other hand, the Shia parties that had thrust their unqualified members in official senior posts weakened the government in a way reflected in the performance of the entire government system. Something else worsened the quality of the governmental system; it was the sectarian quotas that were the cornerstone of the Iraqi constitution. According to this principle, the seats of the parliament had been allocated between two major groups: Shias and Kurds. In the second level, came the Sunnis and secular groups, as well as a few seats were reserved for some minor ethnic groups including Christians. Accordingly, the allied Shia groups monopolized the ministries, so the governmental posts were exclusive to Shia and Kurd Parties, regardless of the qualifications and skills.

The Prime Minister Nouri Al-Maliki, who headed the second allied Shia government in May 2006, declared in one of his speeches that the sectarian quotes even prevented him from choosing the qualified crew.

The militia of the youth religious leader Moktada Al-Sader was quite weakened after many armed clashes occurred in 2008 between his gangs (Almahdy army) and the government forces. These clashes took place in Al-Sader city, eastern Baghdad, and in Basra, second largest city south of Iraq. Consequently, the government forces could exercise their authority in some Shia cities, which already had proved their loyalty to Moktada Al-Sader, expelling a lot of his armed followers to Iran and arresting the others. In any case, the popularity of Moktada Al-Sader as a religious leader was still considerable within these cities. Al-Sader, after the great military failure of his gangs, chose to dwell in Iran, giving his orders from there.

Also, a noticeable fissure developed between the two main allied Shia parties: Islamic Supreme Council and Islamic Dawa party; the reason was seemingly the policy of the Prime Minister Al-Maliki, the secretary-general of the Dawa party, who continued to impose his dominance at the expense of his partners. Many southern tribes and clans that had been devoted to Islamic Supreme Council changed their loyalty to Al-Maliki. If truth be told, these two major Shia parties always had been rivals since the time they were refugees in Iran. But now, Islamic Supreme Council, as well as other partners, accused Al-Malikithat he had the tendency to be a dictator, while they refused singling out the state in one person, such as what had happened in Iraq during the reign of Saddam.

Al-Maliki 's political foes believed that he would like to present himself as a strong leader, able to enforce law and order throughout Iraq, especially after the armed clashes wherein he had defeated Al-Sader's gangs. But they alleged that he used his authority in an unfair and despotic way; they mentioned so many prisons and detention camps which were crammed with innocent people who were held in prison for mere suspicion, even without judicial proceedings. Meantime, the relation between Kurds and Al-Maliki was tense as a result of the transgression of Kurd supremacy on Kirkuk, Khanaqin, northeast Baghdad, and some parts of Nineveh, which met great objections from Arabs. When Al-Maliki made an effort to impose his authority on these territories, the Kurdish military force (Peshmerga) prevented him from his goals after short military skirmishes took place in Khanaqin in September 2008. General Ray Odierno, Commanding General of the U.S forces in Iraq, revealed in January 2010 that in order to ease tensions between Kurds and Arabs, units began the coordination of the U.S military forces, in conjunction with Peshmerga and the Iraqi army in the disputed areas in northern Iraq. All these conflicts reflected the life in Iraq

Even now, several years after the liberation of Iraq, all the basic needs of civil life are still missing. People have suffered for long years from lack of electricity, sewers, and fresh water; and while the corruption in official circles is blamed as the main reason for this failure, the government claims that these defects are a result of lack of security. After Somalia and Myanmar, Iraq became the third country in highest prevalence of corruption, according to a 2010 report of Transparency International, a German organization that tracks corruption across the word every year.

In Kirkuk, life became increasingly difficult than it was before, and the attacks of Arab insurgents against the Kurdish force still troubled the Kurdish leadership. Although all Arabs and Turkmen in Kirkuk do not want their city to be joined to Kurdish territory, the Kurdish leadership still persisted that Kirkuk must be part of their region.

Ali and I kept in touch as he set eyes on my house till the early 2007, when I lost contact with him as he had passed away; he was found dead in his car while refueling in one of Kirkuk petrol stations. His son told me, in one of the calls I made, that his death was the result of a heart attack.

As a result, my house in Kirkuk was not watched over until 2009, when I found someone to look after it, but the problem became more complicated after I was told that a Kurdish man was squatting there and built a fence around it to dwell in.

Since 2006, thousands and thousands of families in Baghdad have been driven out of their houses by the orders of various militias. While the Shia militias did their dirty work of terrifying the local Sunni population to leave their suburbs, those where the majority was Shia Muslims, Al-Qaida, and some Sunni gangs behaved just as badly in the Sunni suburbs. Many reporters for Arabic media mentioned that these militias, who terrified and

killed people, could be controlled because they had committed all these crimes openly, but it looked like no one
wanted to interfere and stop these things. As a result, an
entirely new image of Baghdad City is being shaped in a
way that it had never been before, especially after the
massive walls that were built surrounding some Sunni
suburbs to prevent the incursions of terrorists.

My brother Hisham, after receiving many threatening
messages from one of the Shia gangs, had to sell his
house hastily and move to Mosul City, in northern Iraq,
where Sunnis are in the majority.

My cousin Yousef, who had been kidnapped in Hu-
sayaba, before being able to finish building his house,
had been forced to move to Mosul too.

My brother-in-law Salim and my sister sold their house
and abandoned Iraq to live in Egypt with their children.
They had thought that they would be the last Iraqi citizens to want to leave Iraq, but life became unbearable
because of the regular intimidations of Shia militia, which
had always been accused of being sponsored by Iran.

My brother Sami escaped from Iraq as well, to settle in
Syria. He was unable to sell his auto-wreck spare parts,
which were always a heavy burden that prevented him
from leaving Iraq early on.

My mother, after she sold her apartment, moved to
Mosul as well. She wanted to be close to my brother Hi-
sham, so she leased a small house to live with my brother
Mohammed, and his third wife.

My sister-in-law Radyia and her large family managed
to leave Iraq for Jordan. In one of my phone conversations with her, she said that, despite the hardship of
unemployment in Jordan, her husband Suhail was happy
to live far from Iraq and he had become much less fearful.

As of November 4, 2006, the UNHCR estimated that
1.8 million Iraqis had been displaced to neighboring
countries, with nearly 100,000 Iraqis fleeing to Syria and
Jordan each month.

People left their houses, memories, and dreams in order to reach the western world where a stable and secure life would be offered to refugees, but unfortunately, most of these counties shut the doors against them as their lands grew full with refugees.

It is a fact that refugees who fled from Iraq were not exclusive to one sect or group; that thousands of Shia families shared with Sunni brothers the same fate.

Christians in Iraq also had their lot in suffering. From the beginning of the invasion of Iraq in 2003, radical Islamic groups, like Al-Qaida, looked at Iraqi Christians as "crusaders", the expression referring to the historical religious wars. Accordingly, serial explosions targeted churches in Baghdad and some major cities. Meanwhile, a flood of Christian refugees had to leave Iraq to settle in different countries around the world. In 2009, deliberate attempts were made to drive Christians out of their native city Mosul (Nineveh). Many obscure assassinations using pistols fitted with silencers targeted Christians; the victims were not prominent figures but ordinary people. As a result, thousands of Christian families fled away to neighboring frontiers. It looked like these assassinations had to do with the election as a plan to prevent Christians from using their right to vote. This opinion was strengthened by the fact that all these incidents took place in December 2008, before the municipal council's elections were held, and before the main elections in 2010. Although the Pope denounced these crimes, as did some politicians in Europe, yet the government was not capable to reveal the investigations that were held by a governmental senior committee but the file was closed for doubtful reasons without disclosing any information.

Many years had passed since the floods of people fled away from Iraq to seek refuge in other countries, but the Iraqi government seemed unable to solve this problem. But what about refugees who could not flee out of Iraq and had to escape to adjacent suburbs or cities within

Iraq? This problem still exists and lies on the governmental office desks without any hope for a solution. Local TV channels even now feature the daily suffering of thousands of refugees who could not return back to their homes as a result of sectarian violence in 2006. Some of these families continue to live in tent camps that were set up by the government; and this was the only thing that had been done to solve the problem of these people.

16 Iraqi Elections of 2010

With intensive rivalry, many candidates proceeded to Iraq's 2010 elections, but only huge blocs or coalitions were able to stand up till the end; so that four major political blocs were the main poles of the Iraqi 2010 elections. The Kurdish bloc was represented by the two main Kurdish parties—PUK led by Jalal Talabani and KDP led by Massoud Barzani. This Kurdish coalition gained 43 seats, out of 330 seats. Besides the Kurdish coalition, there were some small blocs that arose in this election, like "The Mass Change", a new party led by Nushirwan Mustafa, the former deputy secretary General of PUK. Nushirwan, who won 8 seats, separated from PUK after repeated calls to reduce the power of the president Jalal Talabani.

Supervisors noticed that Nushirwan's popularity increased at the expense of his foe Jalal Talabani's, who had fallen back a little bit in the polls. This fracture in Talabani's party can be seen as a prominent development in the Kurdish political scene.

On the other hand, it looked that the tribal loyalties in Kurdistan were much stronger than political devotions and the winds of change did not affect Massoud Barzani, as he collected the high numbers of votes in Kurdistan region.

The second bloc was the "State of Law", led by Al-Maliki, which won 89 seats. This bloc had started in 2005 as one of many allied Shia parties, but finished as a single Shia party (Al Dawa) surrounded by some allied Sunni figures. This fact reflected the great fracture that had developed between Al Dawa party , led by Al-Maliki, and the other partners. Al-Maliki's slate proceeded in six provinces in the Shia-dominated south and a little ahead in the religiously mixed city of Baghdad.

The third bloc was the "Iraqi national coalition", formed by the "Islamic Supreme Council", led by Amar Al Hakim, the "Al-Sadr movement", led by Moktada Al-Sader, "Iraqi Congress", led by Ahmad Chalabi, besides some other Shia groups and figures. The coalition was the substitute of the old Shia alliance, which had consisted Al-Maliki party. This bloc scored the third position in the elections after winning 70 seats, and it was leading in populous Shia cities, as well as some parts of Baghdad. More than 40 seats of this cluster bloc were won by "Al-Sader movement". It was an indubitable fact that the religious factor was the main reason for preceding the slates of "state of law" and " Iraqi national coalition" that, despite of hard living and unachievable government's promises, Shia weren't able to cross with their religious references.

The fourth bloc was the "Iraqi List", led by Allawi. It was formed by the "Iraqi National Accord", led by Allawi, the "Iraqi National Dialogue", led by Saleh Almutlaq, the "Renewal List", led by Tariq Al-Hishami, the vice-president, and others from prominent Sunni, secular, and liberal figures. Mr. Allawi was chosen to be the leader of this slate, which won 91 seats in five Northern provinces with large Sunni populations that were once hotbeds of insurgence.

Some Observers believed, in spite of all that happened after the elections, that the remarkable result of Allawi's list changed the political balance in Iraq such that it can be described as a reward for the U.S. policy in Iraq. To understand this issue, we have to look at the evolution of Sunnis' situation through the whole political course in Iraq. One of the aspects of this evolution was the birth of a new moderate political movement "Renewal" led by Al-

Hishami, the vice-president and former secretary general of the Islamic party. AlHishami, who separated from Islamic Party, chose to align with Allawi, the liberal figure, to compose a liberal Sunni bloc. The great success gained by this bloc was being able to quench the power of the fanatic sectarian Sunni movement, the prime adversary to the American existence in Iraq. The fanatic Sunni movement this time claimed only 6 seats, compared with 25 seats that were won by the Islamic Sunni coalition in Iraqi elections of 2005.

Observers believed that Sunnis, most of whom boycotted the elections in 2005, entered the 2010 elections at the full weight, after they realized that there was no way they could set themselves free from their ordeal except through the ballot.

The spectacle now is pretty different from the 2005 elections in that the Sunnis became the preeminent bloc after they aligned to choose a liberal, secular leadership representative in Mr. Allawi.

But, on the other hand, these changes in the political map led to complicated difficulties in forming a new government, especially in choosing the position of the prime minister, even though the election result was revealed in March 2010.

Maysoon Al-Damalogy, the spokeswoman for Allawi's List, summarized the problem in July 2010, declaring to the Arabic Al-Shark Alawsat newspaper that "The problem facing the political process is not to give our coalition constitutional rights to form a government," referred the issue to sectarian reasons, "which obstruct Allawi from commencing his duty to reform a new government."

Al-Damalogy made a comment saying that the other parties look at Allawias a head of a Sunni Arab List, believing that Sunnis should not outweigh Shias, regardless of the constitutional rights of the Iraqi List.

Even before revealing the elections' result, Allawi announced many times that the government of Al-Maliki struggled to keep a tight rein on power, using all illegitimate ways, like cheating, bribing, or terrifying people not to vote to other candidates from other lists. In an interview for BBC on the 17th of March 2010, Allawi said that some helicopters were seen spreading pamphlets over Azamiyah (key 7 in Baghdad map), where the majority is Sunni, inciting people not to vote for Allawi's List, while some local TV channels broadcast many interviews with people from Azamiyah, confirming this fact. Allawi considered this act as law-breaking and asked to launch an investigation. A week before the elections, Al-Maliki was seen handing out thousands of guns to tribal leaders in a bid to win votes, in which allegations of vote-buying and exorbitant handouts grew widespread. Iraqi media showed many photos of Al-Maliki handing out guns to his supporters in southern Iraq, attempting to imitate the image of Saddam.

Allawi declared on many local TV channels that the candidates of his bloc underwent extensive maltreatment and harassment by the government.

Even three weeks before the elections, a decision was made by the "Accountability and Justice Commission", the new name for the "Debaathification Commission", to exclude Saleh Almutlaq, the main ally of Allawi, from the political process, accusing him of cooperating with Al Bath party. Despite the fact that there were many appeals to review the decree (Joseph Biden's plea was one of those), the decision was not changed. Knowing that Al-mutlaq was one of the Iraqi parliament members who frequently objected over the extension of Iranian influence in Iraq explained why he was not welcomed in the new parliament.

Al-Maliki also tried in vain to exclude the Iraqi refugees around the world from voting, guessing they would not vote for his List. However, with all these attempts, and although the power was in his hand as being the Prime Minister, Al-Maliki could not win the required majority of seats to renew his position for another four years. Unwilling to accept defeat so easily, Al-Maliki tried his best to obstruct the way of his foe Allawi, thus circumventing the elections' result.

A few weeks after election, the senior court in Iraq (under the influence of Al-Maliki) issued a new interpretation to one of the constitution's articles, which stated that a coalition formed after the election result also had the right to assign the next Prime Minister. Conveniently, this ignored the fact that time had expired to register these newly formed blocs by the independent High Commission for Elections. Thus, the new interpretation opened doors wide open to the other Shia blocs to reform and coalesce in a single, greater block, seizing Allawi's right. The interference of Iran was very apparent in this game, especially after a meeting had been held in Iran for Iraqi Shia groups who were summoned after the elections, calling them to reconcile their disputes, and amalgamate in one great bloc.

Al-Maliki tried in every possible way to prolong the period before the due date of validating the elections' result by the senior court so that he would have enough time to settle his differences with the other Shia blocs, especially his antagonist Al-Sader, which are the main allied group groups in the "Iraqi National Coalition". Thus, manual counting was one of these means to win more time.

When Al-Maliki was preeminent in the early stages of the elections, he was holding off Allawi's accusations, advocating the integrity of elections; but when the victory was apparent for his foe, he began to challenge the result, calling for re-counts and hand counting.

However, the manual re-count did not change the elections' result; more than two months post-election and on account of the frequent demands of Al-Maliki's List, the decision has been made to go through the re-counting, but the order was confined to the Baghdad district's ballots. Once again, the result of the manual counting was roughly correspondent with the previous result, and the "Iraqi List" remained—capturing 91 parliamentary seats compared with 89 for "State of Law".

In the meantime, the negotiations between the two main Shia blocs—"State of Law" and the "Iraqi National Coalition"—took a long time before announcing the birth of a new alliance, but the new union was to be stillborn as it soon disintegrated again when the "Iraqi National Coalition" sternly refused to accept Al-Maliki to be on the top of the new government; on the other hand, the "State of Law" persisted not to nominate anyone except Al-Maliki.

Al-Sader made a comment in July 2010 to the Al-Baghdadia Iraqi TV channel that he was still having good relations with many members from "State of Law", who in turn revealed that no one of the them was able to propose any other name but Al-Maliki; Al-Sader hinted at the fear that Al-Maliki put in his followers' hearts as a dictator.

Yet, all the attempts to unify these Shia blocs went in vain, and after two months of intense negotiations, they confessed hopelessly that no agreement could be held with the persistence of "State of Law" to nominate Al-Maliki solely as the next Prime Minister. Al-Sader movement was the main opposition to nominating Al-Maliki.

During this period, there were also side negotiations between the "Iraqi National Coalition" and the "Iraqi List", and also, there were other negotiations between the "State of Law" and the "Iraqi List". But, it looked as if the two Shia blocs had entered these negotiations with the "Iraqi List" separately to pressure each other, aiming to get some concessions.

In a late dramatic change, Al-Sader, while dwelling in Iran, consented to nominate Al-Maliki, submitting to the will of Iranian President Mahmoud Ahmadinejad, who is enthusiastic to renew the mandate of Al-Maliki one more time.

However, the Iraqi political scene grew more compli-

cated when the "Islamic Supreme council", led by Sayyed Ammar Al-Hakim split from the "Iraqi national coalition" to take the side of the "Iraqi list". In his weekly speeches to Iraqi cultural forum in Baghdad, Al-Hakim proved to have a lot of liberal attitudes—underlining the importance of the reconciliation between all Iraqis and rejecting the policy of unilateral debaathification.

So far, both sides, the "State of Law" with Al-Sader or the "Iraqi List" with Al-Hakim need the voices of the Kurdish bloc to meet the bare minimum to form a new government. On October 2nd, 2010, Iraq entered the *Guinness Book of World Records* for the longest delay in forming a government[12]. The previous record had been held by the Netherlands since 1977, which was 208 days between an election and the formation of a government.

The U.S. administration tried to engender a compromise between Iraqi disputers, so officials kept stressing on the impartiality of U.S., and assured that it stands at the same distance from all parties. Many observers believed that it would have been much more effective if the government of U.S. had used its influence to put pressure on the different Iraqi parties to get some concessions that might help to form a new government.

Even with the frequent visits of Senator Joseph Biden, the scene was disappointing to those who had hoped to end the post-election deadlock. The relaxed attitude of Washington toward Iraq's crises showed disinclination to get involved; meanwhile it undertook to withdraw its troops from Iraq. Observers believed that while the U.S. was alert to perform its job with impartiality, Al-Maliki (sustained by President Ahmadinejad), took its attitude for his advantage excessively, clinging to his position, hindering any attempts to choose another prime minister. Even on the subject of referring Iraq's crises to the Security Council, Al-Maliki exhibited his refusal to any foreign

---

[12] "Iraq breaks record for longest time with no government." *The Washington Post*, October 1st, 2010

interference, despite the fact that Iraq is still under international trusteeship.

It is not a secret to reveal that the U.S., which sustained Al-Maliki's plans to build Iraqi forces as part of its commitments to consolidate stability and security in Iraq, unintentionally helped to breed a new tyrant able to exploit the fragile security situation as long as he can seize half the people of Iraq. Conforming to the determination of U.S. to fulfil the military withdrawal, Senator Biden showed undisturbed reaction, despite the near standstill in reforming a new Iraqi Government. "Even if the parties are unsuccessful," he said, "Iraq's interim government is functioning well."[13]

Today, the US government gambles with Iraq's stability by turning a blind eye to Al-Maliki's internal policy, especially after Wikileaks revealed his complicity in death squads. We are jeopardizing the hard-won political gains that the US achieved by neutralizing the Sunnis of Iraq when it converted them from fighters and boycotters to voters. The US administration fails to show much real concern for the future of democracy in Iraq except perhaps for its anxiety about Obama's promises of military withdrawal.

Issam Jameel

---

[13] *The Nation*, May 2010

About the Author

Issam Jameel was born in Baghdad in 1954. He obtained a bachelor's degree in theatrical arts from the Academy of Fine Arts in Baghdad in 1978. In 1980, he spent his compulsory army services working for *Al-Qadesia*, a daily newspaper of the Iraqi army. He explored the amazing world of writing when he wrote articles in theatrical criticism. After several years, he became the dependable theatrical critic in *Al-Thawra*, the  main official newspaper in Iraq during the years 1981 to 1985. His first book, which included two plays about war, was published in 1983 by the main Iraqi governmental publishing house. His first play, *The Memory of a Dead Man,* was directed by himself with an experimental theater belonging to a national theater group in Iraq. Three of his plays have been directed by Iraqi directors for the national theater group in Baghdad during 1985 to 1991, while two other plays have been directed by himself at the experimental theater in Baghdad in 1989 and 1993.

He continued his study for a Master's degree in theatrical studies to graduate in Baghdad in 1990. His thesis contained a sociological study about converting the Elizabethan symbols in *A Midsummer Night's Dream* to modern symbols, which materialized in the Iraqi understanding of the play.

Because of the strict limits on liberty in Iraq, he moved to Jordan, where he found a permanent job at a radio station belonging to one of the Iraqi opposition groups against Saddam.

During his long residence in Jordan, he converted to Christianity before migrating to Australia in 2002, where he now resides.

Appendix: Maps and Photographs

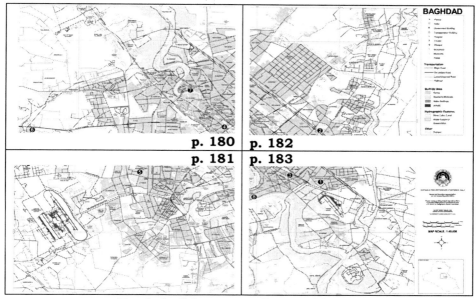

Baghdad (source: NIMA 2003)

Key to Baghdad map on p. 184
Iraq Maps pp. 186-187
Photos of Baghdad on pp. 189-198

Color printable maps at www.IraqThruABulletHole.com

Websites of Interest

http://www.nationalgeographic.com/iraq/
http://www.geocities.com/iraqinfo/
http://en.wikipedia.org/wiki/Iraq
http://www.cfr.org/publication/8429/iraq_timeline_200
5.html
http://pipl.com/directory/people/Caritas/Jordan

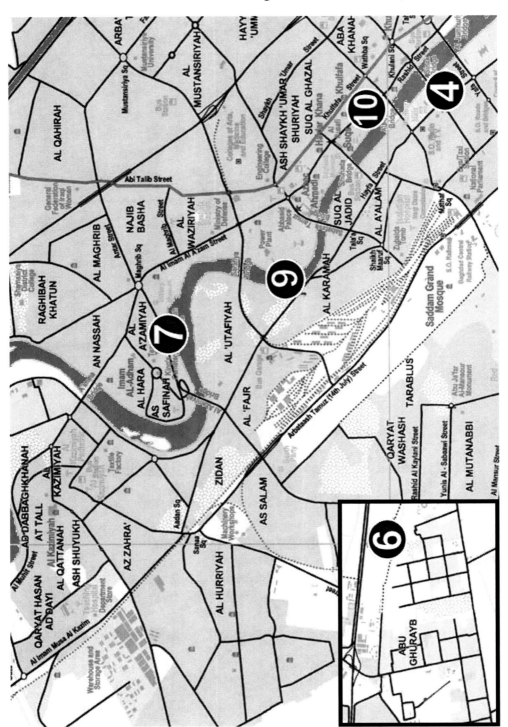

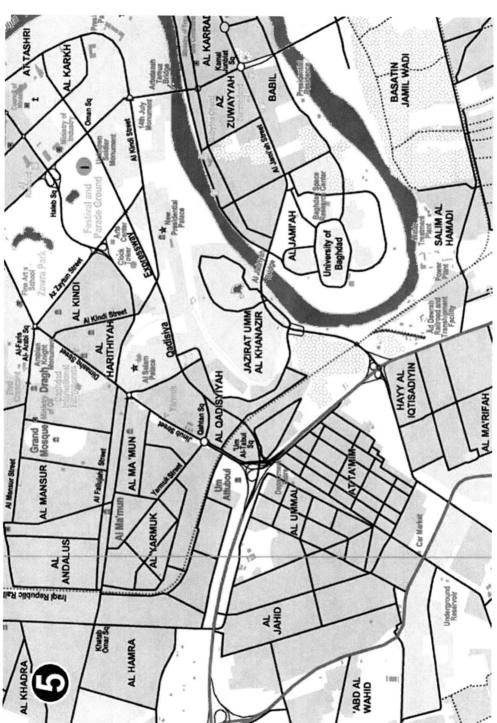

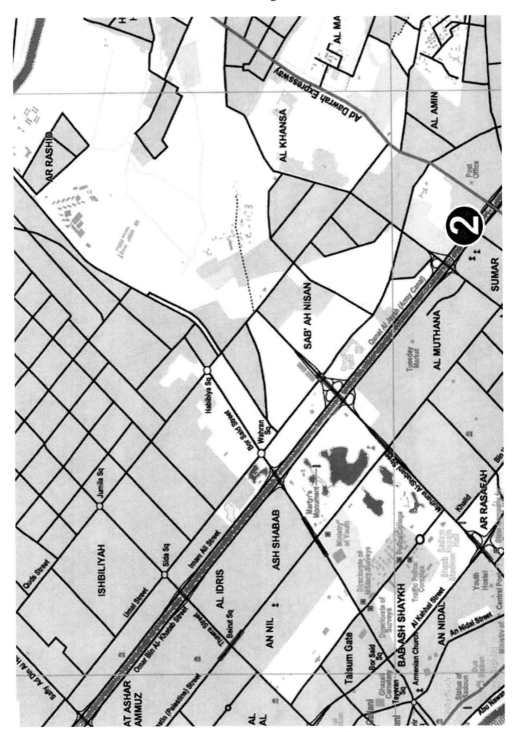

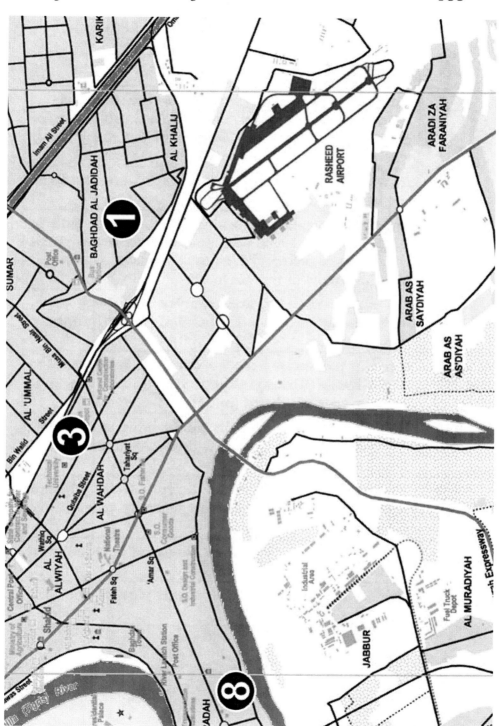

Key to Baghdad Maps (pp. 180 - 183)

①	New Baghdad (Baghdad Al-Jadidah)
②	Channel Street goes parallel to the channel on both sides of the water. Qannat Al-Jaish is the local name and means "Channel of the Army" as it was built by the Iraqi Army many years ago.
③	At the University, the streets were worse and the car barely moved (p. 94).
④	The car crossed the bridge to the other side of Baghdad while I was still looking back to the ruins of the place where I'd spent the most wonderful working times of my life (p. 26).
⑤	My expectations to face troubles increased, especially on the main road which led to the Jordanian border (p. 91).
⑥	I finally realized where we were; we were close to Abu-Ghraib (Ghurayb) district, about 50 Km west of downtown Baghdad (p. 21).
⑦	Habbib chose to cross the next bridge to the eastern side of Baghdad, into Al-Adamia (Al-A'zamiyah) p. 87.
⑧	The landscape of Karada district is magnificent with the Tigris River curving sharply to embrace the palm trees (p. 86).
⑨	Dijla River (Tigris) divides Baghdad into eastern and western halves (p. 25).
①⓪	Rashid Street where the cover picture for this book was taken.

Key to Iraq Maps (pp. 184 – 185)

①	The bus stopped in Tuz Khurmatu city, 80 Km from Kirkuk (p. 108)
②	Many relatives had to stay in my brother's house since they had come from Mosul (Nineveh), one of the largest cities north of Baghdad (p. 41). *Nineveh was mentioned in the Bible when Jonah refused to obey God to go to this city and was subsequently swallowed by a whale.*
③	The car had to use the northwestern route, passing through Tikrit, the city of Saddam's birth. The main road to Kirkuk was blocked by the Kurdish forces (p. 118).
④	The car left the road to park at a rest stop with a restaurant, about 160 Km from the border (p.18)

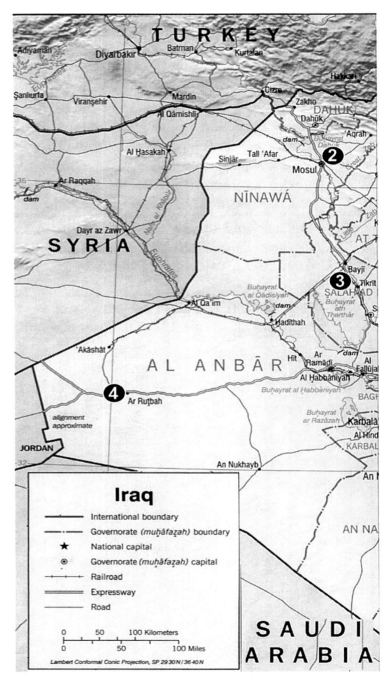

Al-Jamhuria St. in the main market area of central Baghdad

Open markets in one of Baghdad's suburbs
Photos by Ghassan (February 2004)

**A government building demolished in mysterious circumstances
after the invasion of Iraq in 2003.**

Photo by Ghassan (March 2004)

An old lane with traditional houses in Baghdad.

Photo by Ghassan (March 2004)

**Al-Matahaf square and bus station in western Baghdad
(March 2004)**

**Saddam Mosque in western Baghdad. (Feb. 2004)
Photos by Ghassan**

A lane in one of the poor suburbs in New Baghdad (Feb. 2004)

Photo by Ghassan

The Battle for Baghdad (08/12/2004)
"A pair OH-58 Kiowas circle above Haifa street firing Hydra
rockets and .50 Cal MGs, providing cover for the Bradleys of the
Iraqi and American forces on the ground (top). A secondary fire
burns behind the Al-Mansour hotel Simultaneously in Sadr City
(bottom), a secondary fire burns from a previous assault just as
another explosion erupts near a police station." Photos and commentary by Bill Evans.

Green Zone car bomb (07/14/2008)

"The clear morning quiet was shattered by an enormous blast that came at about 9:20am. It was so powerful that it shook the Palestine Hotel where I was staying over 3 Km away.

Shaking from the adrenaline, I ran to the balcony and got this first of a series of shots of the mushroom cloud and then the black smoke from the cars that the blast set on fire.

The explosion occurred at the Rasheed entrance to the green zone. The main entrance for vehicular and pedestrian traffic, it provides access to the headquarters of the Iraqi Governing Council, the Baghdad Convention Center and the Al-Rasheed Hotel (the large building directly behind the cloud). This is the entrance I primarily used to visit those very places.

It is situated at one of the busiest intersections in the city and, if not for the fact that it is a holiday keeping many people at home today, the casualty count would have been terribly worse. News reports put the bomb was estimated at 500Kg, killing 10 and wounding 40 people.

Photo and commentary by Bill Evans.

Rocket attack at 7am (07/02/2004)

"The view from my balcony right after the second rocket hit a car in the parking lot of the Baghdad Hotel some 200 meters away. There were two injuries in this explosion. The smoke from the burning car ended up enveloping my hotel and filling my room with the stench of burning gasoline, oil and rubber.

The first rocket hit the Sheraton on the opposite side of my hotel, striking the 10th floor hallway on the north side.

The improvised launcher mounted in a minivan that was carrying an additional 7 rockets malfunctioned and exploded. It burned next to the mosque across Freedom Square from the Sheraton and Palestine hotels. Although it wasn't reported, shrapnel from the exploding multiple rocket launcher (one piece) hit my hotel, piercing three tempered glass windows on the ground floor."

Photo and commentary by Bill Evans.

Al-sinak communications tower (01/21/2004)

"View from Al-sinak Bridge towards the second largest telephone exchange in Baghdad supplying some 20,000 customers. Those customers, by the way, are back in service today through the efforts of many foreign and Iraqi workers.

The Al-sinak tower, which once belonged to Uday Hussein, today is a wonder to look at. It took a couple of Tomahawks fired from U.S. warships right to its midsection and, as can be seen here, it is amazing that it hasn't just fallen in on itself."

Photo and commentary by Bill Evans.

Al-Mamoun communications center (10/25/2003)

"The tower at Al-Mamoun communications center in the Al-Mansour district in Baghdad continues to stand as a reminder of the former Iraqi regime. Often seen as a background image and a vision unto itself, Saddam's tower remains intact after receiving two direct hits of precision enhanced bombs (JDAMs).

This photo offers a unique and rare view, looking out from the base of that tower, through one of the holes made by one of those two bombs, onto the compound guarded by US troops and beyond to the headquarters of the Iraqi National Congress."

Photo and commentary by Bill Evans.

Index

LaVergne, TN USA
28 February 2011
218265LV00002B/27/P